# Praise for *Respecting Auti.*

Dr. Tippy's compassion and passion ⟨D1198681⟩ tory. I applaud him and his team in their ⟨...⟩ labels to understand and respect each child as an individual with a unique profile of strengths and challenges. Having the opportunity to read Dr. Stanley Greenspan's insights is a real treat, making this very readable book a fitting tribute to him and his important work.

*Paul B. Yellin, MD, FAAP*
*Director, The Yellin Center for Mind, Brain,*
*and Education*
*Associate Professor of Pediatrics*
*NYU School of Medicine*

This introduction to the Developmental, Individual Difference, Relationship-based model (DIR) is beautifully written, clearly presented and reader friendly. Dr. Tippy engages the reader from his first sentence as takes us on a journey into a variety of fascinating case studies of students who have benefitted from DIR intervention. An overview of the underpinnings of developmental approaches, and in particular, the DIR model, is presented through several studies. The text should prove useful to parents, practitioners, and graduate students in related fields.

Case studies are presented to illustrate and highlight strategies to encourage development of functional abstract knowledge through the use of relationships. Insightful detailed reporting enables Dr. Tippy to demonstrate how DIR can empower children to connect and transfer information to broader higher levels. The studies illuminate successful strategies for working with children on the Developmental Spectrum—where children are respected and their thoughts and feelings valued.

Methods advocated in this invaluable new text put back the joy in teaching and learning.

*Dianne Zager, PhD*
*Michael C. Koffler Professor in Autism*
*Director, Center for Teaching & Research*
*in Autism*
*Pace University*

# Respecting Autism

*The Rebecca School/DIR Casebook*
*for Parents and Professionals*

# Respecting Autism

## The Rebecca School/DIR Casebook
## for Parents and Professionals

### STANLEY I. GREENSPAN, MD
### GIL TIPPY, PsyD

*While this book is based on and presents clinical observations and conclusions, it is not intended to replace the advice given to you and your family by your own physicians and other caregivers. The information in this book is drawn from specific cases (names and details have been altered) with a view to general applicability, but neither the authors nor the publisher or their respective affiliates provide any guarantee as to relevance, suitability, or efficacy. The publisher, authors, and contributors expressly disclaim any liability in connection with the use of this book.*

*Cover design by Victor Mingovits*
Vantage Press and the Vantage Press colophon
are registered trademarks of Vantage Press, Inc.

419 Park Ave. South, New York, NY 10016

Manufactured in the United States of America
ISBN: 978-0533-16454-7

Library of Congress Catalog Card No: 2011914455

0 9 8 7 6 5 4 3 2 1

To my wife, Meg, and my two children, Glenn and Sarah, whose love and support have made all of my work possible.

—Gil Tippy

# Acknowledgments

I want to thank Michael Koffler and Tina McCourt, who had the original vision and who gave me a chance to help create this amazing school and all of the things that went with it.

Particular thanks goes to Alla Sheynkin, MS, ED, who read all of the early drafts of this book, offered feedback on whether the book was true to DIR and told the story of the work we were doing, and wrote and rewrote passages of the book where they needed to be more authentic to our actual work. She is the creator of the program we came to call, "Taking DIR to the larger ecological context," and was one of the original pioneers of the school. Without her, much of the good work described in the book would not have taken place, and the transformation from theory to actual classrooms would have been infinitely harder.

I want to thank the staff of the school for their tireless dedication and hard work. They provided the material for the book, and indeed, do the work about which I had the luxury to write. But foremost, I want to thank the parents and the children who attend the school. Thank you for entrusting your most precious gifts, your children, to us, and thank you for allowing us to share your lives, every day, and in the pages of this book. We will continue to try to be worthy of the honor you do us.

# Contents

# Foreword

Since 1985, I've dedicated my life to working with children with special needs and their families. These tireless efforts have made a clear and undisputable difference for thousands of children, a direct result of a dedicated staff focused on an individualized approach to serving each child, carefully tracking progress and honing in on the successful intervention techniques.

In 2003, our organization, MetSchools (www.metschools.com), opened Aaron School (www.aaronschool.org) to serve a population of youngsters with speech and learning disorders. Named after my father, Daniel and Brian's grandfather, it began as an elementary (K-5) school and has now matured to a K-12 program. One particular group in the school was deemed to be in need of a more specialized environment. As a result, in 2006, along with my sons Daniel and Brian, we opened Rebecca School (www.rebeccaschool.org), named after my mother, Daniel and Brian's grandmother. Our mission, then and now, is to create a program that focuses on the strengths of each child, and to craft a curriculum around their abilities and interests, to bring out the best in each one. We adopted the Developmental Individual Differences Relationship-based (DIR®) model, developed by Dr. Stanley Greenspan, a pioneer in the field of Autism. This methodology is based on the core belief that relationships are the foundation of learning—and to spend a day in our world, the meaning of that statement becomes crystal clear. Tina McCourt and Gil Tippy, Program Director and Clinical Director, respectively, deserve an almost impossible amount of credit. Their expertise, care, and single-minded determination have proved that what we are doing works. We have witnessed undeniable progress in our students over the past 5 years; if measured in children's smiles, our success is off the charts!

1

Our intent in publishing this book is to share with the world some of our experiences—the processes, the results—in an effort to bring to light the amazing work that Dr. Greenspan started and Tina, Gil and their remarkable staff continue to move forward, as well as all of the children and families who have benefited from this approach. We dedicate this book to all of you. Furthermore, we hope this starts a dialogue amongst professionals, interested parties, and everyone in between. Your questions allow us to dig as deep as necessary, with the goal that no child leaves our doors unprepared for the world that faces them.

—Michael, Daniel and Brian Koffler, June 2011

# Introduction

In this introduction, I am going to try to explain why I only use the Developmental, Individual Difference, Relationship-based (DIR) model when I work with people on the Developmental Spectrum, as well as when I work with parents and others in my private practice, and with my own children. In the interest of full disclosure, I need to tell you that I was once an "Applied Behavior Specialist" in a group home run by a large agency, and I was responsible for the behavior management of the consumers in that group home. I fully understand learning histories, reinforcement, operant conditioning, punishment, and reward. I actually got trained in the Applied Behavioral Analytic intervention by some highly qualified, famous people in the field. (Although, I am sure they would cringe to acknowledge it now!) However, even while employed as an Applied Behavior Specialist, I always worked in a relationship-based way, never put in punitive consequences to try to decrease a behavior, and did not allow staff to withhold events or activities from consumers as punishment for some action. The staff would howl at me that there had to be "consequences" for the actions of the consumers, but I always understood this as the staff's desire to punish what they saw as unacceptable behavior. I believed it was my mission to help these consumers live richer, more varied mainstream lives, and so I always tried to create interventions that were relationship based. Over the years, the staff got it, and I think the house ran very nicely without token economies or check-sheets and timers. We built relationships.

In order for you to understand why I have chosen DIR for my work, I will have to explain to you why I do not use the Applied Behavioral Analytic model (ABA) in all of that work, and to do that, I will have to explain what I know about the ABA way of working. Remember, this is me talking about an intervention in which I was trained, but which I have chosen not to use, so I am not going to do a good job making you believe it is the right intervention to use. If you want to be convinced of ABA's usefulness or efficacy, there are an almost infinite number of resources readily available to you. That's not my job here; my job is to explain why I don't use it with kids, why I do use the DIR model, and why you should too.

First, let's look at the ABA model. Simply, ABA practitioners will say that if you want a kid, or a guppy, or an amoeba[1] to do more or less of a certain action, you either reward or punish that action. The proof, for them, that you are rewarding or punishing the action is if the action increases or decreases. For instance, if you want a child to point to a red square on a paper, you tell him to, "Point to red," and if he does it, you give him something he wants, an M&M or a Cheez Doodle, for instance. The theory is that if you pair something you want a kid to do, whether he wants to do it or not, with something he wants, then he will do the thing you want him to do to get the thing he wants. This is the Premack Principle, and much of ABA depends on it. So, kids will work for M&M's and point to red. If the amount of times that he points to red when you ask him to goes up, that's proof that the M&M is rewarding, if you believe the theory.

Now, suppose you are trying to get the child to stop pointing at red (nonsensical, I know). You could accomplish this by punishing the child when he points at red. You can either do something to make the situation noxious to the child, behaviorists call this "positive punishment," or you can take something away from the child that he wants. Behaviorists call this second option, this taking away something the child wants, "negative punishment." If the number of times the child points at red goes down, then that is proof to an ABA therapist that what you are doing is punishing, or at the very least, not rewarding.

---

1 I'm not kidding about the amoeba! I was recently at a conference where the speaker, a behavioral researcher, said that his favorite research subject was the amoeba, because they were easy to understand, and they acted just like human beings!

Does this intervention work? Well, that depends on who you ask and what your goal is. If you want to decrease behaviors you can see on the outside, like hand flapping, you can generally do that in the classroom or the clinic where you can have enough control. Will the child continue to be hand flapping free in the wider community? That is not so clear. Whether the child will do what you have trained him to in your carefully controlled classroom when he is out in other situations or with other people is generally said to be an issue of "generalization," a bit of jargon that means, "Will the child, or amoeba, do in other situations what I have trained him to do in my classroom/laboratory?" ABA has some real trouble here, as many of the interventions depend on control of the environment. What you can get a child to do in carefully controlled, and unnatural, environments does often not translate to other situations. For instance, you can get a child to point to red fifty times in a row in a lab, but if you ask that same child whether he wants a red or a blue scarf at Macy's, during the Christmas shopping season, he may have no idea what you are asking him, as this does not match up with the controlled, "Point to red. Good pointing to red!" that he has been drilled on. What's missing? The abstract understanding that things can be different colors, that you (the child) might have a preference, and that your mother, standing before you is actually trying to honor your autonomy and preferences by asking you what color you prefer for something you are going to have to wear on your body. She might have better results, and it would look scientific, if she said, "Point to red." and held up the two scarves, but that wouldn't really accomplish the task, would it?

To talk about why the ABA training fails so miserably in the above example, I need to talk about the core deficits of Autism Spectrum Disorders, and the DIR model. Because for me, the key to why DIR is effective in the face of just this type of situation lies in its unparalleled ability to move kids from dependence on their memories into the rich world of abstraction. You cannot be a memory-based intervention, like most of the behavioral interventions, and somehow magically think this will eventually translate into abstraction. You need to actually address movement into this world, and DIR does that. So, let's next look at what the actual core deficits of Autism Spectrum Disorder are.

As a psychologist, I look to the *Diagnostic and Statistical Manual of Psychiatric Disorders*, the *DSM IV, TR* for my definition of Autism Spectrum Disorders and their symptoms. This book is the authority used by many related mental health professions, is relied upon by insurance companies for payment, and is generally agreed on as a good place to find standard descriptions of disorders that have been generally agreed upon by the community. Whatever its weaknesses, it will stand as our authority here. This latest version of the *DSM* lists Autism Spectrum Disorders separately, although the word is that this will change in future revisions. For purposes of figuring out what the core deficits of ASD are, I will use the diagnostic criteria for Autism, as this seems to me to be the closest disorder to our topic.

In this big thick diagnostic manual, on the pages describing Autism, you will have a hard time finding any mention of the external characteristics of the disorder. What you see, again and again, are social criteria. For instance, the very first criteria for the diagnosis of Autism that is mentioned is a social criteria, "Marked impairment in the use of multiple nonverbal behaviors such as eye-to-eye gaze, facial expression, body postures, and gestures to **regulate social interaction.**" (The bold italics are mine.) So, the very first criteria in the diagnostic manual is not about flapping or other stereotypic behaviors; it is about social interaction. Notice that they mention "eye-to-eye gaze" as a nonverbal behavior that may be missing in Autism, but they put it in the context that the eye-gaze is not being used to regulate social interaction. Typically, human beings use their eyes to regulate the social space between them and the other person. If I were standing in front of you now, I could make eye-contact with you, you would look back at me, and we would begin to have a social interaction. Nowhere does the *DSM* imply that kids with Autism won't look at you, it says they don't use the eye-gaze to mediate the social space. So, the intervention you want is not to tell the kids, "Look at me. Good looking at me!" and then reinforce it, the way they might in an ABA intervention.

The intervention you want should address the core deficit, the social interaction. By the way, you often see studies that say they prove some behavioral intervention works because they have improved eye-gaze. This is nonsense, because you can make anyone look at you, but it is an entirely different thing to help someone with ASD to use eye-gaze the way it is used typically between two people, to mediate the social interaction.

Go through the rest of the criteria in the manual, and you see phrases like, "failure to develop peer relationships appropriate to developmental level," or, "a lack of spontaneous seeking to share enjoyment, interests, or achievements with other people (e.g., by a lack of showing, bringing, or pointing out objects of interest)." Autism is a disorder of relating and communicating, and not a disorder of extinguishable behaviors, and persons with Autism do not have bad memories, as a diagnostic criteria. If anything, they may be using their finely honed memories too much, to compensate for their difficulties with abstraction. So, any intervention that focuses on memory skills, or on discrete behaviors is not attacking the core deficits of the Autism Spectrum Disorders. Difficulties with relating and communicating are the core deficits of Autism, and if your intervention does not take them as the direct target of your work, then you are not doing the most appropriate, relevant, evidence-based intervention. You may have evidence that your intervention correlates with some external behavior, but your evidence is not relevant. We, in the Autism treatment community, would be better served if we changed the emphasis from "Evidence-Based Practice," to "*Relevant* Evidence-Based Practice."

"Evidence-Based Practice" is the drumbeat these days in the behavioral world. It is the way that ABA therapists convince people that their way is the only way to work with kids on the developmental spectrum. They point to mountains of "research," studies where they change some external part of behavior, hand flapping for instance, by some reinforcement procedure. They cannot point to any actual long-term change in the core deficits of Autism, the deficits in relating I just told you about, but they do have mountains of charts and paper. Today, when we have become so enamored of "science," and believe that it somehow will always work to our benefits, we desperately want to believe that this mountain of data will somehow help us out of our Autism crisis. The therapists doing it are sincere in their beliefs, and they bring a zealousness to their work that is hard to beat.

The "Evidence-Based Practice" label appeals to legislators as well. They are frightened all the time, worried they will vote for something that will be held up as a terrible error in judgment in their next re-election campaign. I am writing this introduction in January of 2011, and we see all around us the dangerous results of this endless fear and attack in our political campaigns. Of course, if someone comes to a legislator, no matter how savvy, and tells them that they should be backing Autism research, a real no-brainer, but that they must only back treatments that are evidence based, then they will always take the approach that is least likely to come back to haunt them in a future campaign. "I am a friend of Autism, a friend of the largest fund-raiser in the field of Autism, and of course, I would only back the way of working with our children that has good, hard scientific data to back it up!" That is an unimpeachable political position, but it is dead wrong. The politicians, and indeed parents and clinicians working with children with Autism, have been sold a bill of goods. It is science, it is rigorous, but it is wrong, doesn't treat the core deficits of Autism, and does harm. I do not wish to do harm to kids I am purporting to treat.

I want to be on the side of this debate that respects children. That treats children in the way that loving parents have treated children since man first walked upright. I want to be on the side of this debate that believes that children have feelings and thoughts, and that those feelings and thoughts are at least as valid as the feelings and thoughts of any adult. I want to be on the side of the debate that asks children what they want, that asks permission before we wipe a child's nose, that does not rush. I want to be on the side of the debate that believes that thinking is the work. I do not want to be on the side of this debate that plans to ignore children, that disrespects their basic humanity. I do not want to be on the side of this debate that punishes children by doing something to them, or by taking something they love away from them. There is never any excuse to commit acts against children. Hiding behind a technology, or a philosophy, to commit acts of aggression against children is only the basest kind of cowardice, and I am proud that DIR, and Rebecca School, stand on the side of humanity and right!

A couple of years ago, I was a part of a working group that was writing the mission statement for Rebecca School. I took the task of correlating our thoughts and trying to put them into writing. I think this sums up my feelings about the differences between ABA and DIR.

"At Rebecca School we believe that everything we do originates with respect. Respect for the children we serve, respect for the staff with whom we work, and respect for the families of the children. Respect means to us that we believe that the children have feelings and thoughts that are at least as valid as ours. Respect means that we allow the children the time and space to lead us to where they need to go. Respect means not hurrying. Respect means that we will create the space and the time for the children to work at their pace, in their own unique ways. We show this respect in the relationships we attempt to foster with the children. We put these relationships at the center of our program because we realize that we are serving children with disorders of relating and communicating, and that these are the core deficits of those disorders. When in a relationship with a child, we will always let that relationship take precedence over any schedule, adult need, or final product. We recognize that we are active participants in the relationship, and will always try to keep the respectful relationship going, eventually helping children to become active members of a larger community. We are dedicated to the DIR model, and we do not support teaching or therapy models at variance with that model. For example, we do not support models that punish kids, that assume kids cannot do things, that coerce kids or force compliance, or that do the work for the kids. We see behavior as communication, and will try to understand children, coming to each situation with curiosity and a lack of preconceived certainty. We assume that others are working sincerely, and want to treat children as we say we would like to. We hold the highest standards for the kids, believing that all kids can grow and develop. These high expectations are the structure for the school, and form a framework for the joyful, respectful, rigorous, thinking-based curriculum."

I write this all in January of 2011, after having come back from the beautiful eulogy that T. Barry Brazelton gave at a conference honoring his friend Stanley Greenspan. I am inspired to say all of the above in writing, entirely without the permission of Dr. Greenspan, so I want you to know that this entire introduction is mine without his input. However, I can tell you that one of the last things Dr. Greenspan ever said to me was, "You have to make sure that the good guys win. The good guys have to win." This book is one part of that attempt on my part, and this introduction is a part of the effort. Next, I will explain the DIR model.

## The "D" in DIR

DIR is a developmental model like all the developmental models you have studied in your high school, undergraduate, and graduate classes. Like Piaget or Gesell, it comes from the well-established tradition in Psychology of looking at how humans develop and how that development can go wrong. It is a stage model like most developmental models, and while it allows for some movement up and down the developmental milestones, for the most part, each milestone builds on the one before it. So the "D" in DIR is for Developmental. The Developmental milestones listed below are one version of the milestones first created by Stanley Greenspan, MD, the creator of the DIR model, and later contributed to by many others, most prominently by his longtime collaborator Serena Wieder, PhD.

The Functional Emotional Developmental Milestones:

I    Staying calm and regulated, and shared attention
II   Engagement and relatedness
III  Basic intentional interaction and communication, five to ten circles of communication
IV   Problem solving, co-regulated interactions with a continuous flow

## (Where the Action Is!)

V    Creative and meaningful use of ideas and words
VI   Building logical bridges between ideas

---

VII  Multi-causal, comparative thinking
VIII Gray-area thinking
IX   Reflective thinking with a sense of self and internal standard

I drew a line after the first six milestones, because every kindergarten in this country assumes, and sadly most nursery schools now are in an ill-conceived rush to "teach" kids, that you have reached FEDM VI before you enter. If we can get our kids to the sixth level, they will do fine in school and life, and so we focus on these first six.

Also, I stuck the phrase "Where the Action Is!" between FEDM IV and V, because it has become clear to me over the course of the last five years at Rebecca School, that the jump from being able to problem solve in a continuous flow with another, to using abstraction, demonstrated here by the ability to creatively use ideas and words, is where the real action is in Autism interventions. Virtually any Autism intervention, delivered by good-hearted persons, with good intentions, can get kids to FEDM III. I really believe that a great Floortimer can get most kids to FEDM III the first time they meet them. Most interventions spend their entire time, a child's lifetime, getting to FEDM III, but then, the child still has all the core deficits of Autism. Of all the interventions I have seen, DIR is the only one that recognizes, and directly, aggressively addresses this all-important leap to abstraction, and has real success getting kids to make the leap. Aside from being the humane, developmentally appropriate intervention that it is, it is also effective at moving kids from the world of memory, to the flexible, rich, functional world of abstraction.

Milestone I: Staying calm and regulated, and shared attention (0–3 months). In parenthesis at each level I will put when a neurotypical kid reaches the milestone, roughly. This first level is where a newborn gets organized. No one sleeps in the house of a 0- to 3-month-old. But, as their neurological systems begin to get organized they become calm and available. Regulated is a word we use a lot in DIR, and it means available to interact, neither too low nor too high. In working in the DIR model, you need kids to be regulated, so that you can work with them developmentally. So, if a kid is not regulated, you can't work on answering why questions, or work on shared social problem solving, or anything else. It makes sense, you can't work on your taxes if you're furious at your partner for something, or if you are asleep. Kids can't work at higher developmental levels if they aren't regulated.

Milestone II: Engagement and relatedness (2–9 months). If a kid is calm and available, then we can work on engagement. To be engaged, in the DIR sense means to be related to another, not engaged in some self-absorbed interest. We want kids to be engaged with us, we want to be the most fun and interesting thing in the world. Our goal at this level is to get kids hooked, and we will use the engagement and relatedness to build on the child's developmental milestones within the relationship we are creating.

Milestone III: Basic intentional interaction and communication, five to ten circles of communication (4–9 months). When you offer some communication, and a child accepts your offer, that's a circle of communication. You open a circle verbally, gesturally, maybe with a glance, and you can close them just the same ways. It doesn't matter. This is the beginning of a real conversation, the opening and closing of circles, where I'm really thinking about you and you're really thinking about me. Since the core deficits of Autism are all about social relationships, this is where the work on those core deficits begins to become apparent.

Milestone IV: Problem solving, co-regulated interactions with a continuous flow (9–18 months). This, and the following, level is where the real action is in Autism Spectrum Disorders and the DIR model. At this level you need to be able to open and close sixty or more circles of communication, you crunching what's in the kids head, the kid crunching what's in your head, in a continuous flow. You know when you are in a continuous flow; you will feel it. You know that feeling when you are talking with someone you met at a party, and you are on a topic you both like, and you feel heard, and time passes without you noticing; that's continuous flow. Conversely, if you are at the same party with a different person, and the conversation lags, and you look for reasons to leave the interaction, "Oh, I have to go freshen my drink," you are not in a continuous flow. This fluidity and connection is essential, as it lays the groundwork for the next level, the essential level where kids enter the world of abstraction.

Milestone V: Creative and meaningful use of ideas and words (18–30 months). In a word, abstraction! This is the level that you must get to if you are to enter a world where you don't have to use your memory to navigate the world. Kids on the spectrum have great memories. This is a gross generalization, but I am trying to make a point. They are using their memories to navigate the world, because they are not able to form symbols in their heads, they have not entered into the world of abstraction. Think about it. How many of you know kids on the spectrum who can tell you the arcane details of things that should not matter, what you wore the first time they met you, every word of a Disney movie, etc.? They are using their good memories to negotiate the world, because **Autism Spectrum Disorders are not disorders of memory!** No intervention aimed at memory tasks is useful in attacking the core deficits, relating and communicating.

If you are operating out of your memory, you could do fairly well in school until the middle of second grade. At that point, the curriculum turns from memory tasks to abstraction. In third grade you need to reflect on the reasons for things, and so kids with neurodevelopmental disorders of relating and communicating begin to fail. A developmental pediatrician who sees lots of kids on the spectrum came up to me after a talk and said, "I never realized before why so many of my referrals come at the beginning of third grade!" This is the level at which you can begin to answer emotionally meaningful "Why" questions, and when you get here you are off and running.

How you get to this level is the subject of many books, and you will see in this book how we try to get there. For me, this level is the key, for when you reach this level you take off, and begin to experience the freedom of the world of abstraction. Most interventions can get compliance, but DIR is the king of getting kids into this rich level of involvement with their worlds and the worlds of others.

In my own training, the work, writing and lectures, of Serena Wieder, PhD, have really helped me in my understanding of how to help children move from memory to abstraction. The many times I have seen her talk about fantasy play have added light and heat to my work with kids at this level. I refer you to her work, as it seems to me she is one of the real experts at the work of getting kids to be able to think abstractly.

Milestone VI: Building logical bridges between ideas (30–48 months). At this level, you can take what the teacher is saying at the front of the class, think about it, add it to your thought, and put it back out as a new mix of both your teacher's and your ideas. You need to be able to do this to function in the typical classroom, and if you are not there, you will really struggle. This level is the result of strength at all the previous levels.


### The "I" in DIR


"I" stands for Individual Differences, and in DIR, individual differences in the way the kids process the world is key. That is why you will find so many occupational therapists who are conversant with the DIR model. The transdisciplinary nature of the DIR model is one of its great strengths. Every one of us has differences in the way we process the world. I may like a loud rock concert, you may avoid loud places. Derek Jeter may be able to quickly process visual stimuli, create a motor plan, process feedback from his vestibular and proprioceptive system, and make a throw to catch a runner, whereas I would get hit in the face by the same ground ball. Differences in sensory systems are the norm, or else we would all be playing shortstop for the Yankees. If we allow that all of us have sensory processing differences, why wouldn't we allow that our kids do also? DIR pays particular attention to each child's sensory processing differences. It is one of the most important features of the model, and it is one reason why this model succeeds where others fail. Imagine what it must be like for one student of mine who cannot process visual information with fluidity, so the world appears in flashes, cannot tell where her body is in relationship to gravity, cannot tell where her arms and legs are at any given time, or where the boundaries of her body are. Life for her must be like being thrown out of a plane, at night, in a thunderstorm. How can you work on anything with this child if you don't address her sensory processing? The DIR model is particularly strong here, and it is a part of the model that the average person, and the average therapist, knows little about. I will leave descriptions of how to work on these systems to the volumes of writing that already exist about it, much of it in the occupational therapy literature.

## The "R" in DIR

"R" stands for relationship based, and everything in the model is done in the context of a human relationship. This is how human beings evolved, how human beings have treated their children since they first stood up, and is currently backed with good neuroscience. Humans develop in the context of a relationship, first with Mom as they harness her executive functioning during the first three months of life (look back at FEDM I), and then in their surrounding human community. In this model, everyone needs to think about personal variables they bring to the relationship with the child. They need to think whether they like one emotional state over another one, whether they like boisterous play more than quiet, or vice versa, and whether what is going on in their lives is impacting their relationship in the moment. This model is difficult on practitioners and families alike, as there is no technology, no beeping machine, no screen, no clipboard, or data sheet between you and the child. You are the toy, you are the most important thing in the intervention, and it pulls a lot out of you. However, it is the relationship in the DIR model that makes it the most effective, most rewarding, and most evidence based of all the interventions. It is based upon the evidence of at least 10,000 years of documented human history. Kids develop in relationships, this is a disorder of relating and communicating, and so there is really only one sensible, evidence-based way to go.

This intervention needs to be fun and meaningful. If you find yourself generating all the ideas, you are on the wrong track. If it feels like you are dragging the kid, you are on the wrong track. Affect is your greatest friend, your greatest ally, and you need to harness it. Dr. Greenspan always said not to forget "our old friend, affect."

Have fun, be child centered, be curious, and you will be on the right track.

Gil Tippy, January 2011

# Rebecca School

After opening Aaron School, Michael Koffler (CEO of MetSchools) noticed that children diagnosed on the autistic spectrum were underserved in New York. He set out to build a school-age program for children on the spectrum.

In the spring of 2004, he approached Tina McCourt (who at the time was the program director at the Early Intervention Center of Brooklyn) and asked if she wanted to be involved. Tina had extensive experience with DIR® and had been attending trainings since 1994. She had a strong belief that a relationship-based approach was the best way to serve and help children diagnosed on the spectrum relate and communicate. Michael agreed and they set out to design a building and a program that would fully integrate the DIR model.

In December 2004, Michael conducted a focus group with parents to find out what they would like to see in a school geared toward children diagnosed on the autistic spectrum. The group's responses were mainly about the need for individualized instruction and having a staff that was specifically trained in Autism and not just special needs.

In April 2005, Dr. Stanley Greenspan, the founder of Floortime™ , signed on as a consultant to the school. The building was found at the end of 2005 and construction started in February 2006. Tina hired Dr. Gil Tippy and the two became very involved in all aspects of construction and many of the design decisions. This resulted in a state-of-the-art facility that includes large sensory gyms, multiple art and music rooms, large sunny classrooms with smart boards and amplification systems and a rooftop playground.

In the spring of 2006, Gil and Tina began to interview and hire staff, perform assessments and place children in classrooms. The school opened in September 2006 with forty-eight students and fifty-three staff members. Since then the student population has more than doubled and continues to grow each year.

Rebecca School is located at 40 East 30th Street in New York City. Our 60,000-square-foot facility encompasses five floors and sixteen classrooms. Each floor has classrooms situated around the perimeter of the building with therapists' offices and quiet rooms in the center of the floor. The school has two art studios, one for ceramics with a pottery wheel and kiln, and one for all other art mediums. There are also a library and two music rooms. The school contains a large gym with a rock climbing wall, two sensory gyms, and a rooftop playground. Thoughtful consideration of sensory and environmental experience was used in designing and choosing colors and fixtures.

This book was initiated in middle of the third year of Rebecca School's operation. It is intended to describe the incredible effort and devotion of the staff, the parents, and the kids, in the struggle to provide a developmentally appropriate, thoughtful, integrated education. We hope that in some small way it does, and that when you are finished with the book you will have an idea of what everyone had in mind when we set out on this adventure.

## Chapter 1

# I'll Run with You

Kresimir, or Kreso as we know him at Rebecca School, was not well regulated when he came to us. He was wildly reactive to confusing situations, which because of his difficulties processing information was almost any uncontrolled situation. Rebecca School, on the day when we opened, was at the very least not a carefully controlled situation, so we met very few of Kreso's sensory needs. He had not been in school for several years, and the hubbub of our new school, with forty new kids, all with neurodevelopmental disorders of relating and communicating, meeting each other for the first time, made the space overloading for Kreso. He wanted out.

Even at six he was strong and fast, and Tina, the program director of the school, was trying to give him some deep pressure[1] to help him get grounded, but he was punching her hard with his free hand. I grabbed his hand and said his name hoping to calm him, but succeeded only in frustrating him. My most enduring image of our opening day is of Kreso throwing his head back as forcefully as he could in protest, making sickeningly violent contact with Tina's sternum. I heard a thump reminiscent of a baseball bat hitting a watermelon, and looked at Tina to see if she was okay. She gasped that she was (she wasn't), and as she continued to reassure Kreso I saw him

---

1 Tina was giving Kreso a deep squeeze, because we knew from his intake and the application that his parents gave us that he sought deep pressure and relaxed when he got it. We will talk about giving proprioceptive feedback to kids often in this book, as this is one of the ways we often help kids get a better sense of where they are in space.

19

begin to relax. I will never forget that sound, the look on Tina's face, or my understanding at that moment of how scary it must be for Kreso, or any child, to be in a world so overwhelming and unpredictable.

As part of our school program, we were extremely fortunate to have weekly case conferences with Stanley Greenspan, MD, the creator of the DIR/Floortime model. In these case conferences, we brought the treatment team and the family of a child together, in front of the rest of the school, to present their understanding of the child and the treatment to Dr. Greenspan. It was a nerve-wracking experience for the staff, as Dr. Greenspan held them to very high standard, but it was a wonderful opportunity for a family to have direct contact with one of the great minds in child development. We all benefitted enormously from these weekly case conferences, and when Dr. Greenspan followed up with Tina and me the following day, he often really blasted us for the ways in which our school did not reach his high standards. This weekly direct guidance helped to make the school the special place that it is, and formed the core of my own development in the DIR model.

During the case conference for Kreso, his mom was choked up as she spoke about her son's developmental history. English is not her native language, and that, mixed with tremendous emotion, made it hard for her to speak. "When I was pregnant with him I was never sick. He was overdue twelve days. I went to the hospital for a checkup, and the doctor said he was fine. He was a healthy baby. From seven months to nine months he was calling me and my husband." She paused to compose herself. "I'm sorry. When he was twelve months I brought him in for a checkup. I remember much better that day. He was very happy. For one year he'd never been sick. He was beautiful baby, and when he was one we sent him for checkup, you know they gave him shots, you know. He was sick for maybe ten days. But with high fever, you know? Up until one, he was never sick. He never took a Tylenol, Motrin, nothing. After that he wasn't calling me anymore; he wasn't calling my husband anymore. I saw there was something wrong with him. I sent him to his pediatrician and I told him, 'You see, he's more lazy; he's not walking or talking or looking at me. He ignores me.' He said, 'He will be well. When he turns two years.'

He went to early intervention[2], a half day, but he also had therapies, OT [occupational therapy], speech [treatment by a speech and language pathologist], physical therapy, and Applied Behavorial Analysis[3]. He went to two other schools, and now he's here. I feel he is better, but I feel he is nervous, especially at home. He is very nervous, he cries, he jumps, he hits himself, very very badly. He hits his brother sometimes. To be honest, I don't know what to do." She broke down.

On the day I met Kreso he had on overalls and a look of mischief. He looked at the wide open 10,000-square-foot space that we were temporarily in, and smiled. Dad explained, "He loves to run. If it were up to him, that's all he would do. He loves to run. Back and forth." I asked Dad and Mom to play with Kreso with a set of toys I had laid out, and I could see the look of real doubt on their faces. It said, "Are you nuts? He will never play with those things." But they sat down on my little carpet and tried.

The video of that session consists of either Dad or Mom physically wrangling Kreso as he tried to flee to the relative safety of the wide-open warehouse space. They did their best to comply with my apparently nonsensical wish, but just like the opening day of the school, all Kreso wanted to do was escape. Eventually he did, and when Mom and Dad went to speak with Tina, I followed him.

He ran around the space, squealing a high-pitched sound of freedom. He would flop down in an oversized beanbag chair, catch his breath, and then, begin running again. Finally, he calmed, and we sprawled together across the beanbag chair and stared at the floor. I tried hard to figure out what Kreso was interested in, until he reached out and grabbed a little bit of hard cement, and rolled it between his fingers, enjoying its bumps and sharp edges. He held these bits up, from time to time, cocking his head

---

2   Early Intervention is a program in which a school district provides needed services to students in their district before they are school age.

3   Many of these therapies, Occupational Therapy, Physical Therapy, Applied Behavior Analysis, and others are described in the Glossary of Terms later in the book. We use these terms throughout the book, as many of the students have had all these therapies and more. At Rebecca School we provide many of these therapies as part of our transdisciplinary model.

as he twirled them before his eyes, as if trying to find the right angle at which to view them. We lay there blissfully rolling sharp pieces of dried cement between our fingers, sometimes making eye contact, sometimes not, for a while. When his parents returned with Tina, we stood up to greet them. It was only then that I realized that Kreso had wet his overalls through. He had made no indication of need, and still seemed unaware of being soaked.

Kreso fought to get what sensory stimulus he could into himself in a way he could process—whether through running back and forth through the space to try to feel his body, holding things before his eyes at an angle where he could make sense of them, or rubbing edgy stones between his fingers so that he could feel some tactile input. Kreso was a boy with all the perceptual portals to the world blocked and slowed—the doorways were there and he could sometimes see a glimpse of light through them, but they were tantalizingly unavailable to him, just out of his reach. As a result he was always at the mercy of a surprising world which he had trouble experiencing, and which he had no chance of understanding.

This left Kreso unable to calm down and pay attention to things. He spent much of his time just trying to get regulated. He could share attention with someone else, but the activity had to make sensory sense to him. He couldn't share ideas and build on them. I saw no fantasy play that Kreso could share with me, but he could go back and forth for some few circles, sharing his pleasure when he could finally feel something. With little language, Kreso was a roaming muscular boy trapped behind portals of perception that were failing him.

### Sensory and Motor Strengths and Challenges as Understood and Described by the Rebecca School Staff:

*Visual Spatial:*

- Visually sensitive.
- Tends to use his peripheral vision.

- Will hold objects close to his eyes and manipulate them while staring intently.
- Will flap his hand between his eyes and a light source.

### Auditory:

- Easily overstimulated.
- Uses his hands over his ears to block out sound.

### Proprioceptive:

- Uses a weighted blanked for deep pressure.
- Seeks and prefers the Lycra [brand name] swing in the classroom.

### Vestibular:

- Seeks linear as well as rotational swinging.
- Tilts his head back as he swings.

### Tactile:

- Has difficulty standing close to other people.
- Rubs a spot that has been brushed (during a brushing protocol).[4]
- Prefers to be barefoot.
- Has decreased awareness of pain and temperature.

### Feeding:

- Very limited food choices.

### Motor Processing and Planning:

- Severe difficulties in both.

---

4 Brushing protocol: The occupational therapist has followed one of several standard protocols using special brushes on a child's skin. These protocols are designed to help the child feel the limits of his body, and integrate sensations from the outside.

*Integration:*

- Difficulty integrating sensory information.


### Rebecca School Program in Place Before Consulting with Dr. Greenspan

*Floortime: 6–10 x 20 min./day, Individual, primarily in the sensory gym, with teacher or one specific teaching assistant, primarily.*

- Focus on Level I, to help Kreso to stay regulated, and Level II, as Kreso has difficulty remaining engaged without direct adult support. These sessions, and most of Kreso's program, take place in the sensory gym.

*Speech: 3 x 30 min./week, Individual, Oral Motor-Protocol[5] in the classroom.*

- Oral-sensory motor input four times throughout the school day for ten-minute intervals. His oral motor-protocol includes extra-oral vibration to stimulate the muscles of the face and lips and the presentation of a textured chewy tube on his back molars. PROMPT Therapy.

*OT: 4 x 30 min./week, Individual.*

- Most sessions take place in the sensory gym. Focus on Level I, in an attempt to help Kreso stay regulated and available to attend. Vestibular and proprioceptive input. Brushing[6] every two hours in the classroom.

---

5   Oral Motor Protocol: The Speech and Language Pathologist is using a standard protocol with Kreso to help him begin to be able to feel his mouth and the mechanisms of speech and swallowing, among other things.

6   Brushing: This refers to a brushing protocol put in place and supervised by the occupational therapist.

*Music Therapy: 1 x 30 min./week.*

*Art Therapy: 2 x 20 min./week, with two peers.*

## Dr. Greenspan's Recommendations

Kresimir, a little boy who is six years old, has been attending the Rebecca School since September 2006. He has a history of regression in terms of language and engagement beginning at the age of one year, after having been ill with high fever upon receiving a vaccination. Also, he has a history of sensory-processing challenges including sensory regulation. Kresimir will be described in terms of the different milestones to be achieved and his current level of functioning.

Kresimir can be calm and regulated but can get dysregulated especially at home where there isn't the constant sensory support. We need to broaden his ability to tolerate frustration and increase his use of signs, symbols, Picture Exchange Communication System[7], and words. Also, we need to increase his circles of gestural communication.

Kresimir can engage and is very likeable, and it's obvious that he and his mother have a close relationship as well. We have to help him deepen and sustain that engagement even when he is dysregulated. Kresimir can be purposeful and get into two-way communication, with fifteen to twenty circles, but he can't do it across the full range of activities and emotions. A critical goal is to get him into a continuous flow. Work on longer and longer conversations and interactions. Kresimir can do shared social problem solving, but we need to help him do it in more of a continuous flow and in a broader, more flexible way.

Kresimir is in the beginning stages of using ideas, is doing a little pretend play, using short phrases and simple words, but sometimes repeating the last choice. We have to expand his pretend play and use of language.

---

7 Picture Exchange Communication System (PECS): A communication system using picture symbols in the place of words.

The key to expanding the use of ideas is combining text with pictures and words in highly motivating situations in a continuous back and forth flow and having longer and longer dialogues to help him develop more use of ideas. Once Kresimir is using ideas and doing pretend play, we can begin working on making connections between ideas.

### Constitutional and Maturational Variations

Contributing to Kresimir's challenges are difficulties in many processing areas. He has auditory processing and language challenges. He also has motor-planning and sequencing challenges. His challenges in sensory modulation leads to him getting overloaded easily and is also responsible for his being so sensory craving and active. His visual-spatial processing is a strength for him and we want to strengthen it more, and harness it to augment his other areas of processing.

Kresimir's prognosis is best indicated by his learning curve over the next few months and years with an appropriate intervention program. As that curve continues on an upward trend, his prognosis for continued improvement remains very good because of the progress he's already made and the good program he has at school.

### Game Plan:

1. More focus on getting a continuous flow of back and forth interaction going. Within a few months Kresimir should be able to do fifty-plus circles. Also, work on broadening his emotional range.
2. Increase Kresimir's use of symbols by combining words, PECS, and actual pictures with highly motivating activities. Also, do more pretend play using subjects he likes. Have the dolls swinging with one labeled KRESIMIR and the other labeled as his friend. As part of the interaction, he would have the word written under the picture and ask again if he wants to swing or go to sleep. Because Kresimir's

visual-spatial area is strong, using the visual supports should get him into the world of ideas much more quickly.

3. When Kresimir is doing what looks like visual stimming, try to enter his world and see what it is he is looking at to engage him; move it around and see where he wants it to be. Play to his visual pleasure.

4. There needs to be a very close and consistent relationship with the family. It's a much bigger challenge for the family in the evenings because they don't have the staff support and equipment at home. Set up an active program at home that is consistent with what is being done at school. Have intensive meetings and home visits with mother for the next couple of months and then regular weekly meetings.

### Alla Sheynkin, MS, Ed. writes about Kresimir today

Often, when I see Kresimir in the mornings, walking off the school bus through the lobby door and sprinting to his classroom, he is sensorially and emotionally regulated. After two years of attending Rebecca School he can anticipate and adapt to the traffic slowing down his bus ride, to navigating his way through the loud lobby full of excited and animated greetings from staff to the other eighty students coming in at the same time as Kresimir, and to the demands that will be placed on him in the classroom. The demands that are placed on Kresimir can seem small to an average observer—taking off his coat and putting it in his cubby, or not hitting a teacher while he has to wait for her to get the classroom settled to take him to the sensory gym.

In Kresimir's world these demands are anything but small. Without the ability to think abstractly and be able to predict what happens in the future, based on previous experiences (i.e. "My teacher took me to the sensory gym yesterday right when I got to school, and she did say she would take me, but that loud classmate of mine is acting up again, so I think she needs a few minutes to settle him down before she and I can go to the sensory gym again like yesterday."), many children, including Kresimir, either abandon the task and give up, or become exasperated with the perception that their needs will not be met. Similarly, without the understanding of the fact that a coat thrown on the floor will get stepped on, that a new coat would cost Mommy and Daddy money, and that money comes from holding down a job, Kresimir may see the teacher's demand that he pick up his coat as just another nonsensical, pesky request. Since before he turned two, Kresimir has been in different therapies and schools, all oriented around changing his behavior, giving him directions to follow, without consideration of what goes on inside him that leads him to do the things he does. When we accepted Kresimir into our program, we knew that it would be a long and rocky road, but we were committed to walking it along with him. Actually, perhaps running it along with him. Kresimir loved to run, and that was our way in. If we ever wanted him to join us in our world and one day care about the condition of the coat that Mommy bought for him, we should not expect someone with auditory, visual-spatial, motor-planning and sequencing, and modulation challenges to take the first step. We had to meet him where he was. So, an energetic and strong teacher that we hired to work one-on-one with Kresimir started running with him. That was the beginning of their relationship.

Eventually, a teacher running after a student in a playful way leads to the student referencing the teacher, saying, "Hey, I love running and seemingly so does this guy. Wait, is he still following me? Oh, there he goes again after me, I better speed up. Running together is much more fun than running alone!" Soon the student begins chasing the teacher, and later on two students that both love running can learn to run with intent and purpose after one another. That's how one gets into a continuous flow of interactions, starting with the two or three circles of communication that Kresimir struggled to open when we first met him, to twenty, thirty, forty, fifty and so on. And, one day when Kresimir's teacher asks him to hang up the coat in his cubby, he will do it not just because he has memorized the procedure of the beginning of a school day, but because the relationship with that special teacher is motivating enough for Kresimir to do things that are important to another person. Even if Kresimir cannot yet get through a long chain of sequential thinking about why coats need to be hung up, he can relate to his caregiver. He may think, "If it's important to my friend, I will do it, after all he knows how important running is to me."

Chapter 2

# "Neurotic New York Mom" Knows Best

The beginning of the Rebecca School, as I described at length in the previous chapter, was less than smooth, to say the least. On top of our trying to create a program with a group of kids that had never had a DIR intervention before, and a staff only newly trained in the intervention, we also had an entirely new facility. We had gutted 60, 000 square feet of building to the walls, and this included replacing all the windows. Previously, the building had served all kinds of functions, but it had never had a need for secure windows. Apparently, now it did. I was on the sidewalk in front of the school on the second day, when I saw a package delivery guy from one of the big national chains barely miss being hit with what looked like a little missile, in bright primary colors. It hit the sidewalk and sounded like a rifle shot, the guy jumped, and looked up, swearing, trying to figure out where this missile had come from. I knew very well where it had come from, because it was a hard plastic rain stick we had bought as part of some of the classrooms' first-day toy stock. I picked it up (after the delivery guy was around the corner!) and went on a fact-finding mission.

I brought it to a classroom on the sixth floor, roughly in line with what I took to be the path of the projectile (all that watching of forensics shows paid off). I asked the classroom staff, "Do you have one of these?" They said they did. I said, "Let me see it." It was clear to me by the look of urgency, if not panic on their faces, that they understood they had better produce the

30

toy. The head teacher scrambled to the supply closet, rummaged around frantically, and stood up, triumphantly holding the twin to my toy over her head like a trophy. I thanked her and went to the seventh floor.

I knocked on the door of the classroom directly above the one I had just been in. I asked again, "Do you have one of these?" They said they did. "Show it to me." This time there was less scrambling around. It had been out and they had been using it. In fact, Gabriel had been playing with it. The teacher asked his teaching assistants if they had seen it. Then all eyes turned to Gabriel. He looked satisfied, somehow. The teacher admitted that they could not find it, and so I explained the circumstances surrounding how I came to have it in my possession. Gabriel had set if free into the air above the sidewalk in front of the school. The teacher sheepishly took it from me, and I walked out. I turned back to the classroom in time to see the teacher pantomiming to his class, "OH MY GOD!" and holding his head. And that is how we learned about Gabriel, and his desire to make things disappear. It is also how we learned about the need for locks on the classroom window screens.

Mom described Gabriel, "as not being in the mix." She was referring to how she first noticed that he, at eighteen-months-old, was different from the other children on the playground, but it is the perfect description of him now as he walks through the doors of Rebecca School. This strong-willed thirteen-year-old boy, with big blue eyes and long lashes, travels alone. He walks from the bus to the door of the school, makes his way into the lobby and waits for the elevator with the other kids, but he just is not connected, not in the mix. There is a separation to him, a distance that pervades his interactions.

Mom reports that Gabriel made all of his early milestones on time. He spoke single words, but Mom began to notice that he was not putting together two words as some of his peers were at eighteen months. He would initiate actions with the family, was attentive to the world around him, Dad would jingle his keys outside the door and Gabriel would come running, for instance, and so the family was initially happy with his progress. Dad admits now that he was not initially supportive of Mom's concerns, as he saw evidence of Gabriel's intelligence everywhere. Dad says, "There was a little tension there. I didn't think he was developmentally delayed. We were also both concerned that he was going to get a label, at this age, so we probably didn't get him the resources that we could have gotten, because we didn't want him to be categorized at that young an age." Mom added, "It's also a hard thing, as you know, to process as a parent. Very difficult." But Mom had nagging doubts. She took her concerns to her pediatrician who called her a "typical, neurotic New York mom," and told her to go home and love her baby. Luckily for Mom, her own mother said, "That's crap," and told her to get a second opinion from another pediatrician. This pediatrician broached the subject of Pervasive Developmental Disorder with Mom. The doctor suggested that this may be the problem with Gabriel, and although she knew nothing of Autism or PDD, Mom immediately mobilized to get her son help.

She first went to a major New York university's evaluation center to get her son diagnosed. "And quite frankly," Mom says, "they were not that helpful, either." They told Mom that while they felt he was a little delayed verbally, "Boys talk late, so why don't you wait until he is three," to get him services. Mom waited a little bit, but told herself, "This is nonsense." So she took counsel of her better judgment, and swung into action. She took Gabriel to a speech and hearing clinic, and a woman there told her about early intervention. Around this time, Mom noticed Gabriel using "gibberish" between real words, noticed that he would jump when he was excited, and that he was "flapping." Mom says, "Needless to say, I was quite concerned."

Gabriel's original evaluation for OT at the university evaluation center concluded that he did not need OT, as his gross-motor skills were quite good. Again, Mom describes herself as lucky, as she ran into an occupational therapist at her playground, who came to her home and explained to her what Sensory Integration Dysfunction was. "That sounded more like what I saw with my son." He started speech and OT a little after he was two years old, and around three he got a SEIT. Mom credits this SEIT with teaching her how to play with her son, and for supporting her in helping to make her time with Gabriel more interactive. His after-school speech therapist tried an Applied Behavior Analytic approach with him, which Mom says did not work. "One of the things about my son is, he is very strong willed, and if you try to teach him something that he is not interested in, he will completely turn off. He hated it. My husband and I didn't know what to do because we were told, 'This is what you do with children like this.' So I was frightened because I said, 'Well, great, this isn't working.'" Mom was told by that particular therapist, "If you don't continue ABA, your son is going to be a vegetable."

Around this time, Mom read *The Child with Special Needs* by Dr. Greenspan, and attended some conferences, hearing Dr. Greenspan speak. She began to make herself as well informed as she could, consulting DIR therapists, including speech and OT. "I began to see that if I just gave him some physical input, he was a different kid. But if you didn't, he would either retreat, or whine, or cry or definitely not do what you were asking him to do." Unfortunately, consistent school placement was an ongoing problem. Initially, Gabriel's preschool experience was good. The following year, however, the class size, configuration, and teachers changed, and Gabriel was allowed to withdraw into a corner for most of the year. His saving graces this year were the young high school volunteers in the class who drew him out and played with him. On the days when they were in the classroom, Mom says Gabriel had a good day.

The following year Gabriel was admitted to a school, only to be "exmitted" when the school decided that they wished to graduate more children to typical schools. Gabriel no longer fit their newly revamped admission criteria. This left Gabriel without a school. "In March, I had no school, and it was very frightening, because at this point I knew inclusion was not working for my child. We scrambled." They found a placement, in a special classroom within a Montessori school, but it was only adequate, and did not meet Gabriel's need. They found a placement for Gabriel on Long Island, but as they live in Manhattan, this meant a very long bus ride two times a day for Gabriel. This ride, along with the rigidity of the administration of the school, caused the family to continue to look for the right place for Gabriel. They were able to find another school for Gabriel, and get him a paraprofessional to stay with him at school, but after three years he aged out of that school. That's when Gabriel and his family came to Rebecca School.

Gabriel's parents have taken him for extensive allergy testing, and found that Gabriel is allergic to dairy products, soy, purple dye, and wheat. He is on a gluten-free/casein-free diet. Mom tries to limit Gabriel's sugar intake, and makes meals with no processed commercial foods. She makes sure that Gabriel has protein with each meal. He is also taking nutritional supplements including: calcium/magnesium, vitamins C, E, B6, taurine, glutathione, and a probiotic. A neurologist prescribes Trileptal for Gabriel, and he also takes Melatonin before bed, also upon the advice of his neurologist. In February 2003, Gabriel had three grand mal seizures within three weeks of one another. He was hospitalized for one week at a University Medical Center, where they did video/EEG monitoring. Gabriel has not had any seizures since then. In the wake of this episode, Gabriel is taking Lamictal to control seizures.

On meeting Gabriel and his parents, the overwhelming impression was of parents who deeply loved and respected their son. Under less than ideal conditions (our not-yet-built facility, on a one-hundred-degree day, with no air-conditioning and no bathrooms), they got down on the floor and played with Gabriel, following his lead as he lay on the floor and wanted to pretend to go to sleep. Dad got down with him, wrapped them both in a blanket, and began to reenact their bedtime ritual with incredible warmth and understanding. Mom played catch with Dad and Gabriel, again as Gabriel lay on the floor and led the way in how he wished to play. That initial meeting let us know that this was a family that was ready to fully embrace the Floortime and DIR philosophy.

At Rebecca School, Gabriel is in the most diverse classroom in the school, in terms of Functional Emotional Developmental Milestones (FEDM). It is a classroom of twelve- to fourteen-year-olds, who range from two girls who spend much of their time working with the staff to stay focused and regulated at Milestone I, and students capable of extended work at the upper Milestones, including Milestones VII, VIII, and IX. Gabriel falls in the middle of this group. He has islands of capacities at all of the first six FEDMs, and is more or less able to sustain functioning at these levels, depending on the way his sensory sensitivities are affecting him.

Gabriel has a mixed sensory profile, including visual and auditory sensitivities. He is prescribed prism glasses for activities like reading or writing, but he does not like to wear them. Throughout the day Gabriel is always on the move, bouncing on either the trampoline or in his seat. Gabriel likes to look in the mirror—it is apparent that he becomes visually stimulated when he turns his head to the side and blinks excitedly, moving closer and further away from the mirror. He does the same thing when he is near someone he is happy to see; he bounces two or three times very quickly coming close to someone nose to nose, but he knows just where to stop to not touch the nose. That's just his way of saying hello.

Gabriel becomes visibly dysregulated when he is in a noisy environment. Other children's loud screams are not pleasant for him, however other frequencies and pitches seem to be more problematic. For example, if one student is bouncing a ball, another is clinking wooden blocks, another is having a conversation in a moderate voice, and a teacher is sitting right next to Gabriel, it seems that to him all these noises are equally loud and he does not know how to process and organize all of them or on which to concentrate. Often teachers report hearing Gabriel say "fire truck" and about five seconds later they will in fact hear the sirens of a fire truck passing seven stories below on Park Avenue. Gabriel's mother reports that on one occasion he said to her "thunderstorm" and about five seconds later, she did hear thunder.

### Sensory and Motor Strengths and Challenges as Understood and Described by the Rebecca School Staff:

*Visual Spatial:*

- Visual sensitivities.

*Auditory:*

- Easily overstimulated.
- Will request that others stop singing.
- Responds well to low, slow sounds by OT report.

## Proprioceptive:

- Seeks proprioceptive input.
- Will crash into beanbag chair.

## Vestibular:

- Engages in self-rocking.
- Constantly on the go.
- Responds to linear input, swinging, being pushed in a rolling chair.

## Tactile:

- Tactile defensiveness.
- Will "brush away" a spot where he was lightly touched.

## Oral Motor:

- Has limited preferred foods, and has difficulty manipulating food in his mouth.
- Puts nonfood objects in mouth.
- Will swallow large nonfood objects.

## Motor Processing and Planning:
- Good gross-motor skills.
- "Brilliant" at Yoga.
- Difficulty generating new motor plans (will walk around the room without discernible intent.)

## Rebecca School Program in Place Before Consulting with Dr. Greenspan

*Floortime: 4–6 x 20 min./day, Individual in the classroom, with teacher or one specific teaching assistant, primarily.*

### Speech: 4 x 30 min./week, Individual.

- Increasing the number of communication circles per interactive exchange (via words, gestures, or TANGO).
- Increasing the variety of pragmatic functions to include requesting, commenting, and asking questions.
- Improve symbolic and pretend-play skills.
- Making inferences about what has happened or what might happen.

### OT: 3 x 30 min./week, Individual; 1 x 30 min/week, group.

- Therapy has focused on improving sensory processing and regulation, engagement and interaction, language processing, motor coordination, and attention/focus.

### Music Therapy: 1 x 30 min./week.

- Playing instruments for extended periods of time with dynamic range and minimal flexibility with intentionality.
- Singing—exploring sounds while developing and accepting musical/vocal dialogues with therapist (nonverbal).
- Engaging in interactive pretend play, creating brief story lines and/or ideas while being supported by the music based on his interests and passions (i.e., trains, cooking, chocolate).
- Increasing his eye contact and attentiveness as he looks for nonverbal cues from therapist (Gabriel has always shown to have strong visual learning skills, and when regulated uses this as a means of understanding, organizing, and creating meaning of the external world).
- Not only increasing his level of tolerance to external sounds while keeping himself regulated and engaged, but also embracing the sounds and responding to them in a meaningful and communicative manner.

### Art Therapy: 2 x 20 min./week, with two peers.

## Dr. Greenspan's Recommendations

Gabriel's early history was suggestive of a child who enjoyed interaction and who was warm and loving. He continues to be described by his parents as an "in your face" youngster, although occasionally he will make lots of sounds and pace a little bit and he craves a lot of movement. His main challenge appears to be in the area of expressive language, and also in his need for constant movement and certain kinds of sensory input. He also gets sensorially overloaded very easily.

Gabrielle can be calm and regulated and attentive, but he can get dysregulated in busy or noisy environments. He also has a hard time if we're not working with him in terms of his craving for movement. We do better in holding his attention longer and keeping him calm for longer periods when we work with him around movement and around firm, tactile pressure, rhythmic activity, taking care not to overload him and keeping the sensory threshold within his range.

Gabriel is very engaged and that's a real strength of his—he can engage with others and is very likable and has always been engaged. He can sustain his engagement for reasonable periods of time, and we want to help him sustain it for even longer periods of time and more deeply, even when he's getting dysregulated or craves movement, incorporating others into that pattern of re-regulation or moving so that he doesn't have to do it on his own. For example, he can create a sports activity between himself and Mom or Dad or different staff people since he's good at sports, and that way he doesn't have to move alone. When Gabriel is making sounds he can make music and invite others to sing along with him as a way of countering some of the auditory overload.

Gabriel can be interactive and purposeful and get into a continuous flow. Again, we want to extend his purposeful interaction more and we also need to broaden it so it's across a broader range of activities.

Gabriel can problem solve and sequence and, here, too, we need to broaden his problem solving across a wider range of activities and different processing areas.

Gabriel can use ideas meaningfully and tell others what he wants using simple phrases. He can do a little bit of pretending and this is where we see he's at the beginning stages of using his ideas, in terms of simple pretend sequences, rather than grand epic novels. So here we have to enter his drama and create more complex interactions as everybody has been trying to do with him. If everyone sticks to it just at the verbal level it's going to be hard because that's taxing his area of limitation, and although he has an augmentative communication device that speaks, I'm not sure that's the most effective way of working with him since he can speak. He doesn't really need the oral-motor support as much as he needs ways of communicating that take advantage of his strength, which is his visual understanding of the world. We need to figure out how to harness his visual strengths a little bit more in order to help him elaborate in his pretend world more, but that's the goal—enter the pretending, but help him elaborate a little bit more. I'll talk more about that in a minute.

Gabriel can also combine ideas together and connect his ideas to the ideas of others. He can answer lots of "W" questions but he can only answer "Why" questions intermittently. We have to help him master the "Why" level and then get to multi-causal "Why" questions, then comparative "Why" questions, and finally help him get into gray-area thinking, where he can really elaborate and then be reflective; at that point we'll have him at the twelve- to thirteen-year-old level. So, we have a lot of work cut out for us here, but if we harness his strengths in the areas of visual understanding and engagement, he'll make more rapid progress.

Gabriel has some challenges. Among these are challenges in language and auditory processing. This area represents Gabriel's biggest challenge, especially in terms of developing expressive language. He is strong in some of the gross-motor-planning areas, like around basketball and sports. He's a "good shooter," but has a little bit harder time in terms of sequencing, in terms of play themes, and some of the fine-motor tasks, but he's making progress in that area. Gabriel is very sensory overreactive and also very sensory craving, particularly for movement, which goes along with children who are well coordinated, gross-motor-wise. That's one of his strengths, so he likes to use that for regulation.

His visual-spatial processing is also a relative strength for him. He has a good visual memory and we want to help him build on that to be a better visual problem solver, so he can use his visual strengths to think at higher and higher levels and so we can get him to more abstract levels of thinking through that visual system. We don't know how far he can go here—that's a question mark. We know it's a strength, but we don't know how much of a strength, so we have to harness it and see what he can do. Doing just a little bit of the *Thinking Goes to School* program as part of a range of things those working with Gabriel are doing with him may not be quite enough emphasis to really harness this strength.

Gabriel's prognosis is positive because of his strengths in engagement and visual memory and hopefully visual problem solving, which sounds to me like it's there and a potential strength, as well as the amount of language he does have and that's where the major challenge has been, in terms of developing expressive language, but we don't want to let that hold him back too much, so we want to work with it but also around it.

In terms of facilitating Gabriel's progress, which has been good—particularly now that there's an integrated program where home and school are working on the same page, which has been true throughout the course of his development periodically, but sometimes it's not been true—so the approaches that have been taken with Gabriel have been a little bit uneven. So, here's what we want to do to strengthen the program a bit more:

When we're interacting with him we want to keep the circles of communication going and make the interaction more elaborative, but we have to join him in periods of dysregulation. When he seeks movement, that's not a break or a time out. He doesn't need a movement break; instead, he needs someone to move with him. We need to turn the movement into pretending, so we want to take advantage of his strength. He loves gross-motor activity because he's a good athlete, so why call a time-out? We're going to say, "Okay! Should we be horses or elephants or tigers? Where are we going? Oh, you're going to take us to the jungle. Oh-oh. Sounds scary; what do you think?" Let's build the drama with that. Or we're playing a drama around feeding and all of a sudden Gabriel starts moving, we can say, "Okay, we were eating. What are we doing now?" If he can't come up with something, we can say, "Well, are we looking for more and better food or are we looking for a spot to sleep?" He'll probably say, "more and better food." Now we haven't given him the next step in the drama, but we've given him a choice and we're extending the drama. That's the way we extend it when he moves around.

I recommend doing the same thing at home—when he begins moving, we extend the drama. When he starts humming and making sounds or begins pacing and making sounds, yes, it's regulatory; yes, it may be to counter some auditory hypersensitivity—we're not sure exactly what it means to him because he can't tell us yet. He will eventually be able to tell us and that'll be very enlightening. But one thing we can do to help him get to that day where he can tell us is, again, to join him in the making of the sounds and making music out of it, giving him choices, "Do you want me to hum with you or do you want me just to walk with you and be quiet?" When giving him choices, it's not high affect that's important here; it's empathetic affect and a sincere interest in what he's doing. A common mistake everyone makes is that when a child does something very idiosyncratic, we don't approve of it and we don't like it, and we wish the child weren't doing it. A sensitive child knows this. However, if we are a bit "odd," we can really enjoy the child's idiosyncrasies and think, "Hey, I wonder what he's trying to tell me. That's kind of an interesting sound." When we say to a youngster, "Hey, that's kind of neat. How about this one?" and make our own "weird" noises, we create an interaction and start having fun together. So, rather than parroting back what Gabriel has said, I recommend making another sound that's kind of complementary that extends it and, together, we make music out of it. We want Gabriel to be idiosyncratic, unique, and special, but we want him to do so in a social context. What makes someone maladaptively idiosyncratic is that he does it in a way that isolates him or leads to self-absorption. What makes somebody interestingly idiosyncratic and creative is that he does it in a social and interactive context. A new kind of music that, at first, sounds very antithetical or idiosyncratic to all the musicians eventually becomes jazz or computer music, but at first it isn't anything like that. For all we know when Gabriel is making unusual sounds, he's creating pictures in his mind. He's a very visual guy and may be having multisensory experiences. He may be seeing pictures that are quite beautiful and maybe he will tell us about that some day, but not if we don't respect what he's doing. So when we make it interactive we bring it to a higher plane and no longer do we have just unusual idiosyncratic sounds, we have music with his voice. I would bring in, also, musical instruments and work on singing and making different sounds. Initially it can be just different sounds, but we have to counter his sounds with sounds of our own that are interesting to him and that are regulating and not parroting back and that are not with the goal of discouraging him, but to encourage him to do more. Once it's interactive, all of a sudden he'll come to you and want to play the sound game. Then it's no longer self-stimulatory; it's now a new type of music. If Gabriel tries to discourage someone else's singing, it may be because he doesn't like the sound and that he finds it auditorially overloading. In the bathroom he gets more of a mellow sound and more of a resonance and the voice is at a slightly lower pitch, so he may prefer that. But that's what we want to find out. If he says, "Stop singing," parents can say, "Oh, could I try it like this?" and they can do it at a lower tone and experiment until they find something he likes. They could also try instruments, such as the piano or drums, to see what he likes.

We need to increase the time we spend with Gabriel on one-on-one creative interactions in pretending. We want to do Floortime at least six to eight times a day for twenty minutes or more each so we're really getting a lot of opportunity to interact with him. We also want to bring in pictures to the Floortime interactions. To extend the drama, we want to have lots of pictures of all kinds of things available, especially any kinds of themes he tends to develop (around eating, etc.) during pretend play. We'll see if he can use pictures to take the next step. Parents and others can ask him, "What next?" If he can't tell them, they can ask, "Is there a picture that would help?" and they can look at the different pictures together. If he points to a picture, those working with him can have him describe what's in that picture and then jump into the pretending using that theme and that picture. So we need to use pictures to extend pretending.

I would not use the audio box for Gabriel because I want to encourage his talking. The symbol system is helpful to him, but he's not using it that much and rather than wasting time I'd rather we just support him with pictures or, with a symbol board he can use by pointing to a symbol. We also want to encourage him to use typing for written communication. His writing right now is no more sophisticated than his spoken language so it's not a real asset and his reading is not more advanced than his receptive language. If his language becomes more developed, we could use writing and reading to facilitate pretend play and longer conversations.

At home in the evening while Mom and Dad are doing chores they should have elaborate conversations with Gabriel. In other words, the goal is not to have him just be obedient or learn routines or learn that he's a responsible member of the family, although we're including all those things, but as they're doing that they can also incorporate the same things I'm recommending, such as giving him choices and getting him thinking all the time. They can say, "Gabriel, what should we clear from the table first?" "Why that one, why not this one?" It'll make clearing the table a little less efficient, but it'll really be getting his language cooking while clearing off the table; it'll get done eventually but it'll be more fun for him and for the parents. Same thing in the bath: "How do you want the water? Hot or warm?" Parents can put him in charge, so he's giving them directions about how to do these routines that get him ready for bed.

Because Gabriel is a pubescent, emerging adolescent boy, he needs a little more Daddy time, so Dad should get home earlier at least some nights during the week. I suggest getting home an hour earlier three nights a week and catching up on Saturday or Sunday mornings for a couple of hours. Total work hours per week could remain the same, so no total time would be lost, but his schedule is just rearranged because Gabriel needs a little more of him during the week, particularly as he's getting into adolescence. If I have one factor that predicts whether a child with these kinds of language problems is going to get more problematic in terms of behavior, like throwing things out the window, it's not enough time with Daddy. He has to have more time with Dad, just hanging out, having conversations, doing music together, just having fun together and just making the conversation as elaborate as possible. Dad needs to be a "buddy" so Gabriel can identify with him. Because Gabriel's language age is much younger than his chronological age, the more he identifies with Dad by just hanging out, the more he'll be a happy camper and the more he'll also follow the rules and not challenge or become disobedient, so parents will have fewer behavior problems. Spending more time with Gabriel is very vital—it's a very high priority and it's very worth Dad's while in terms of Gabriel's progress, but also for Dad's peace and comfort, especially as Gabriel gets older and bigger.

When Gabriel says, "Repeat, Mom," Mom can "play dumb" a little bit and have fun, saying, "What should I repeat?" If he can't answer on his own, Mom can give him two choices, including what he wants her to repeat, offered first, and then something else, offered second. She can also ask, "Why?" If he can give a good reason, she can reward him. She can also use his request to "repeat" to extend the conversation by asking, "How many times should I repeat it?" "Five." "Five? Why not ten?" "Okay, you asked for it; ten times, Mom." Now they're having an extended conversation generated by his interests, so it's important to turn every interest of his into a long conversation. He's the boss of conversation. Parents are the boss of dangerous behavior, what he eats, and the medication he takes, but Gabriel is the boss of the conversation. Parents and staff should remember that and always try to be playful and respectful around their conversations, and avoid making value judgments. We don't think to ourselves, "This is inappropriate because he's asking me to repeat it and I don't want to encourage that." What happens is that there's a missed opportunity to have a long conversation because that's what he's interested in. Where his interests are is where we're going to get the best conversations. This is the most common challenge we have—taking advantage of the child's natural interests. Even in public it's better to go off to the side and have a conversation than it is to avoid embarrassment. In the long term it would be far more embarrassing to have Gabriel be twenty years old and unable to hold a conversation or answer "Why" questions. That's why it's important to respect what he says and to adjust the social situation accordingly.

It would be better if Gabriel could sleep in his own cot or bed, even in his parents' room. I suggest doing this gradually and taking one thing at a time. For example, parents could put a bed next to their bed so Gabriel has his own bed but it's nearby and he can feel their presence near him. They can gradually create a little more distance and eventually when he's a "big boy" he can go back in his own room, but this must be done very, very, gradually.

Gabriel has an excellent program and is making nice progress, but we want to focus more on a few of the essentials, including extending pretend dramas; extending conversations; and capitalizing more on his strengths in the visual processing and motor areas, as well, by using more visual support, including pictures, and by building movement into verbal interactions. We want to consider everything he does as creative, beautiful, and wonderful, and we want to join in and have fun with what he does and work off of it, versus parroting and modeling. Everyone who works with him needs to keep experimenting until they find a way of extending that he will enjoy; I can't guarantee he'll enjoy it the first time they try, but he will if they keep working at it with the idea of having fun together. If he starts crying, I recommend seeing if he can show through pretend play or with pictures what he's crying about or if he can do so by using words. Parents can rub his back and give him deep pressure. If parents have ideas about why he might be crying, they can offer them as multiple-choice answers. We want to help Gabriel explain and elaborate. He's a youngster with lots of potential. The staff is doing a great job, but I think we can strengthen the program a little bit more. At home, I have the same recommendations as I've made for the staff. Parents are doing great with him, he just needs a little more Daddy time, more extended conversations, and a little more fun with what we would ordinarily call his "idiosyncrasies."

## Rebecca School's Response to Dr. Greenspan's Suggestions

There are kids in every classroom that require a lot of attention caused by their dangerous, aggressive, or otherwise disturbing behaviors. Gabriel is not dangerous or aggressive, and although he can be sneaky about disposing of unwanted items in his surroundings by either tossing them out of the window using his impeccable aim, slipping them down the elevator shaft, or swallowing them, he gets a lot of attention in his classroom because he is just so charming and sweet. Even at his worst moments when he screams or throws himself on the beanbag chair or the floor, he elicits patience, respect, and affection from everyone who works with him. He gets those qualities from his parents, who have always been a pleasure to work with, and have reasonable, appropriate, and meaningful goals for their son.

Gabriel is not yet an abstract thinker, which combined with many sensory challenges, makes him quite rigid. His classroom and home are filled with toys and books, which do not interest him much. Despite the fact that Gabriel likes to pretend-feed us pizza and, if asked to elaborate, can say if the pizza is plain or pepperoni on it, this sort of pretend play is rote and does not develop abstract thinking. Therefore, asking Gabriel to play with toys results, at best, in him acting out someone else's ideas and then disengaging, as that is not interesting to him. Teaching a child to say, "Vroom, vroom" as he holds a truck, is not the same as him deciding that it is a pasta-delivery truck, which is driven by a goat to his grandpa's house. To come up with original ideas and use them creatively, a child needs to first learn to hold images that are not concrete in his mind, think in symbols, and be able to sequence them. Once a child is able to do that he will not need to rely on memory and can be more flexible. So in order to help Gabriel make significant progress, the classroom staff is working on two main goals—longer chains of back and forth interactions and developing symbolic thinking. Whatever Gabriel is drawn to, lining up pictures in a certain specific way for example, his teachers try to intervene, and slowly, smilingly, sneakily mess up the order. The trick is to do it in a way that does not threaten Gabriel's sense of comfort and control, but in a way that challenges his flexibility and stretches it out a little bit at a time. Because Gabriel's teachers and therapists have developed strong relationships with him, they know just how much they can push him on any given day or moment.

Like any teenager, Gabriel is more forgiving of his peers, rather than the pesky adults, so the classroom staff will often ask Gabriel's classmates to do something they know will get a reaction out of him to help him become less rigid. For example, Gabriel always tells adults to "Stop sing, okay." However, recently when one of his music-loving classmates, who sings to everyone all the time, came over to Gabriel with some adult facilitation and performed his rendition of "Twinkle, Twinkle, Little Star," Gabriel listened to it and said "Yeah" once his friend finished. The strained expression on his face suggested that the "yeahing" was a celebration of the song being over, and not his friend's talent, but he tolerated it nonetheless. His musical sensibilities may have been offended, but he is on the road to increasing flexibility. He is on his way to being "in the mix."

## Chapter 3

# Tickle Monster Model

I watch Lydia as she whirls toward the door, bouncing off the bus, full of the joy and smiles that make her popular with everyone she meets, and I reflect on how this little girl has changed over the course of the past school year. Sometimes, it does not seem possible that this bright connected six-year-old is the same child as the limp, disconnected four-year-old I first met. Now she elicits from everyone an enthusiastic, "Good morning, Lydia"; then she very well may have gone unnoticed. Unnoticed, that is, except for her gorgeous clothes that highlight the rest of her natural beauty. She is impeccably dressed, whimsically dressed, always, but before it seemed like she was a static, soft doll; now she appears to be an attention-demanding, eye-catching sprite darting by.

Lydia and her family came for admission to Rebecca School on a rainy summer day before we first opened. She came through the doors in the arms of her mother, who held an umbrella with a long dinosaur tail hanging from it. Lydia, in her green and gold slicker, matched the umbrella, with a stegosaurus's spikes down her back, and even her boots carried on the theme. Within this fantastic fanciful apparel was a quiet, remote little girl. After hanging up all the rain gear, I asked the parents to play with their daughter. They enthusiastically got down on the floor, but they struggled to get her interested in anything they showed her. She appeared determined to ignore then. She had a benign look, a very pleasant, but aloof look on her face, as she looked away with a faint smile. They worked up a sweat, very eager, but became frustrated. They looked at the toys I had offered them, and looked up imploringly because they could not find anything to catch her attention. Finally, when I brought out a hippity-hop, and they plopped Lydia on top of it, we got to see just a glimpse of the bright affect we all have come to so love here at Rebecca School. Her parents bounced her, hard, on the ball, and counted with each jolting bounce. She lit up, and began to vocalize with them, but, as soon as the bouncing stopped, Lydia lost her tone, the affect drained from her face, and she retreated again. She reminded me of newborns, whose parents prop them up between pillows to take a picture. You can see that they are limp, and that without the prop they would fall over. For that momentary picture they look fine, but without the support, their lack of muscle tone and gravity get the better of them.

Mom and Dad took Lydia to see Dr. Greenspan in his office in Bethesda, Maryland. They came back and told us what the experience had been like for them. "It really took so much for us to get down there on the floor, and bring our enthusiasm up to the level it took to really get her engaged. So, after a few tries, we had what we thought was a really good twenty minutes. We were dripping with sweat, exhausted, and we looked up to Dr. Greenspan, and he said, 'That was great! Now you need to do one-hundred percent more!' We realized this was going to really take a major effort on our part."

Mom talks about Lydia's history. "Prior to her second birthday we started to worry. She had had language when she was nine months old, and then she started to regress. By the time we got the diagnosis, Lydia had pretty much stopped talking altogether. When we got the diagnosis, we started a pretty aggressive ABA home-based program. It was over forty hours of various therapies, OT, speech and ABA. That worked okay, we had nothing to compare it to; there was a lot of crying. We were then advised to put her in an ABA-based school the following fall. We did. Lydia pretty much flatlined at that point. We were desperately frightened and concerned. Never had we seen any kind of fantasy play, there was no pointing, the language was a little bit better, but it wasn't increasing at the rate that everyone was telling us we should expect.

"We started to look around at what our options were. We found Dr. Greenspan, and I read several of his books. We heard about the Rebecca

School being formed and got in touch with Tina and Gil. We went to see Dr. Greenspan, and then started trying to implement Floortime within the ABA structure that was part of her day, and that really caused some problems. It was at that time that we started to see some behavioral stuff that we hadn't seen before. Biting her fingernails, and she started biting the inside of her lip, things like that. When we finally got her out of all ABA interactions, and we had Alex Klein[1] coming to the house to help us and our other therapists who had been ABA-trained learn to do Floortime, we started to finally see some pretend play and much more relatedness. It was like she had been underwater and had come to the surface, finally. Then in the fall we started Rebecca School, and have seen definite progress ever since. Nice progress.

"At her very best, Lydia is absolutely on. She'll grab my hand, she'll say, 'I want tickle/chase, Mommy,' she'll call her brother over, engage him in tickle/chase, she's completely present, her eye contact is totally there; it's pretty exciting to watch! She'll laugh, she'll say, 'I want again,' she'll grab your hand and pull you along."

I have seen the tickle/chase game in a video the parents brought in as part of a parent training. It was a dramatic, high affect, squealing, running event, as the name might indicate. First, Lydia looks at her Dad, who put on the face of "I'm about to chase you!" Then, Lydia giggles with a mix of excitement and happy anticipation as she thinks about Dad coming after her. Her body tenses, getting ready to either be tickled or escape, and then she is off! Dad chases her around the circular layout of the apartment until he, Lydia, and the excitement all collide, as Lydia crashes into a soft group of cushions, and the Tickle Monster falls on her tickling and laughing. After the initial excitement, Dad backs away, the hysterical giggling subsides, and Lydia looks up with a mischievous grin. The tension rises, both bodies tense, Dad makes the imminent-chase face, and Lydia is off again! The pattern repeats again and again, always with Lydia in the lead, always with Dad in pursuit. It is a scene I imagine being played

---

1   *Alex Klein:* Alex was one of the founding faculty of the school, and one of the most important guiding forces in our correctly using the intervention. More than any other faculty, I was able to count on his evenhandedness and his deep knowledge of the DIR model when I needed support. Lydia's parents hired him as an in-home Floortime consultant.

out across the world, in every language, wherever kids encounter Tickle Monsters! But, with Lydia, the question is, "How do we get her to chase? How do we get her to initiate?" And, that is the question with many of the kids in this book, in our school, and across the range of neurodevelopmental disorders of relating and communicating.

Mom continues her narrative, "Recently, Lydia commented on something. She was looking out the window, it was pouring rain, and she said, 'It's raining.' And then she started singing the Piglet song, you know, 'Rain, rain, rain, rain, rain,' well I don't know the words, but, we thought that was pretty significant." Dad says, "She also asks for people who aren't there who she wants to see. She might say John, or Joe, or Mommy. Someone who's not there." "Lydia does this whole vamping thing in front of the mirror at home," Mom says with a chuckle. "Literally, she does the posing, she's looking over her shoulder, and there's that big smile. It's pretty hilarious."

Mom speaks about back and forth. "In terms of back and forth, she will answer questions like, 'How are you?' with, 'I am fine.' The other day she asked me, 'How are you?' And I answered, 'I'm really doing great!' But, we are only starting to get a little bit more than this kind of really rudimentary conversation now. I've never heard her answer a "Why" question. She will answer who or what, but I have never had her answer a "Why.""

The parents have also pursued biomedical interventions for Lydia. They have had her scoped throughout her digestive tract, looked at her for gluten intolerance, given her prescription drugs, given her holistic medications, and been willing to pursue every avenue to help her. She had been casein-free and gluten-free, to no effect. Her constipation got worse. "It's been a real crapshoot, helping her," said Mom.

Lydia's mother and father came in for a formal parent training group run by Alex Klein and me. In the group we give a little education on DIR, Floortime, and child development, but mostly we offer hands-on coaching. Then, parents bring in video tapes of a Floortime session at home with their child, and Alex and I lead the parents and the rest of the group through a discussion of the Floortime principles at play, and help the group explore different ideas with each child. During these four sessions, the commitment that Lydia's family has made to Floortime and DIR for her became evident. The family has literally transformed their house into a Floortime playroom, with symbolic areas, semistructured problem-solving areas, and sensory areas. Mom, who did most of the playing for the parent group video tapes, rolled on the floor, dressed up, acted silly, laughed, chased, and wooed Lydia across their house, with an unmatched commitment to the model. It was fun to watch, and the other group members were helped to see how much fun, and work, great Floortime sessions could be. The progress Lydia has made is partially due to her school program, but the level of involvement of this family has made the real difference.

### Sensory and Motor Strengths and Challenges as Understood and Described by the Rebecca School Staff:

*Visual Spatial:*

- Good visual-spatial awareness.
- Visual-spatial processing is a relative strength.

*Auditory:*

- No sensitivities noted.

*Proprioceptive:*

- Enjoys physical activity with proprioceptive input.

*Vestibular:*

- Responds to large amounts of vestibular input.
- Likes to be moved in a lot of different directions at the same time, like spinning on a swing.

*Tactile:*

- When dysregulated, will bite her arm, hard.

## Oral Motor:

- Bites her hands, quite hard at times when frustrated.
- Sucks her thumb.
- Mouths objects.

## Motor Processing and Planning:

- Excellent gross-motor skills, and can use her strength to maneuver objects the way she wants them.
- Recently began two- and three-step obstacle courses.

## Rebecca School Program in Place Before Consulting with Dr. Greenspan

*Floortime: 4–6 x 20 min./day, Individual, in the classroom primarily.*

*Speech: 3 x 30 min./week, Individual.*

*OT: 4 x 30 min./week, Individual.*

- She has a sensory diet that is implemented every hour during the school day.
- Sensory seeking.

*Music Therapy: 1 x 30 min./week, Individual.*

*Art Therapy: 2 x 20 min./week, with two peers.*

## Dr. Greenspan's Recommendations

Lydia, a little girl who is five years old, has been attending the Rebecca School since September 2006. I had the honor of seeing Lydia and her parents last spring. She has a history of being diagnosed with ASD and had some intensive ABA work, which didn't help as much as her parents would have liked. Lydia plateaued in the ABA work and it actually seemed to dispirit her. Since coming to the Rebecca School, she has been making lovely progress.

Lydia can focus and attend. She can get dysregulated, but can refocus. We want to broaden her emotions and range so she can extend her attention and focus for longer periods of time. She can engage, but we want to broaden her range of emotions. She can be purposeful, and open and close five to ten circles of communication, but is not yet in a continuous flow, although we get the sense that she is capable of a continuous flow with the right activity and enticement. This goal is within her reach, and we should be aiming for it to happen in the next three months. At home and school, we want to work on this.

Lydia can do shared social problem solving, but not in continuous flow. She can use ideas, is using short phrases and whole sentences, and answers "W" questions, but not yet the "Why" questions. She has some islands of pretend play, getting into some activities with make-believe, but it is not as extensive as one gets the sense she is capable of. Combining the pretending with the sensory experiences and having her being the pretend character (use costumes, etc.) will help her get there. She is combining ideas, but not at the "Why" level. We want to move her ahead in both Milestones V and VI, by strengthening Milestones III and IV, and getting the continuous flow going.

## Constitutional and Maturational Variations

Lydia has challenges in areas of sensory processing. Auditory processing and language are her greatest challenges. She has relative strengths in motor planning, and we want to strengthen this further to help her be stronger in sequencing many steps in a row. She has trouble with sensory modulation as well. Lydia has mixed reactivity in that she is both over- and underreactive. There are sensory experiences that she does like, and we can use these to help her organize and regulate, and to be less frustrated.

Visual-spatial processing is an area of challenge for Lydia, and it is very important to understanding her difficulties. This area has not been tapped in Lydia as heavily as it could be. If we can strengthen that system, she can begin to see the whole forest instead of just the individual trees. Use searching games, treasure hunts, tracking exercises, and a lot of physical exercises involving perceptual motor and balance and coordination activities. Whenever a child is more obsessive and ritualistic, we always want to broaden that visual-spatial system. Once we get her into a continuous flow and better language capabilities, then we can do the *Thinking Goes to School*[2] exercises with her, maybe in the next six months.

Lydia's prognosis is best described by her learning curve over the next few months and years with an appropriate intervention program. As that curve continues on an upward trend, her prognosis for continued improvement remains very good. She shows lots of strengths and is coming into her own now. She is beginning to use her mind more as a symphony rather than just piecemeal. This is a good prognostic sign for Lydia.

## Game Plan

1. *Continuous Flow/Floortime.* The key for Lydia is to get her into a continuous flow. This will require a little more one-on-one work with her throughout the day. Increase her Floortime sessions up to about six to seven one-on-one sessions where everyone is working on getting the continuous flow. At least half of those sessions should be oriented toward imagination, using costumes, mirrors, etc. The way to get her over her more rigid side is to tap into her imagination.

---

2 *Thinking Goes to School:* A book by Harry Wachs and Hans Furth, is a book we rely on heavily at Rebecca School. It outlines a set of exercises we use, and have modified over the years, to help get children's sensory systems working together. The full reference is provided at the end of the book.

Take advantage of her interest in riding the bus and build around that, for example.

2. *Thinking Skills.* We want to move Lydia ahead in her thinking skills. Within the next month, she can probably begin to answer "Why" questions with multiple choice help (good choice first, silly one second)[3]. Create highly motivating situations, like wanting to swing, and give her multiple choices about why she wants to swing. This will open her up a little bit more.

3. *Rhythmic Activity.* Do a lot of rhythmic activity with music, dancing, playing the bongo drums, etc. Make it fun, and let her warm up at her own pace. Movement and rhythmic activity will be good for her. This should be part of Lydia's daily program, at least an hour a day every day doing all the things she enjoys at home.

4. *Home Floortime.* At home, try to make the time you have with her in the evening part of Floortime activities. Make sure you have a lot of good sensory equipment available at home.

5. *Biting, etc.* I think the hand biting, frustration, and rigidity are all tied together. The rhythmicity, continuous flow, etc. will be the antidote to these things. Broadening her range and getting her more flexible will help. Start introducing the word "anger" and other emotion words during Floortime sessions to help her express herself more.

Again, the main thing for Lydia is to get the continuous flow going, use more imagination, and begin answering multiple-choice "Why" questions. She is coming into her own and this is wonderful to see.

---

3    This seemingly simple instruction is the brilliant way that Dr. Greenspan always suggested to help parents and therapists work with children who repeat the last thing said. By offering them the choice they do not want last, and giving it to them when they echo it back, parents are quickly able to help their children through their echolalia. It also has the additional positive effect of honoring the child's language as meaningful, and that leads in the direction of the child coming to understand, on a deeper level, the meaning of language.

## Chapter 4

# Squeals of Laughter

I don't think I've ever had more fun with a kid on first meeting him in a testing situation than I did with Lenny. In walked this very quiet, reserved mom, with this quiet, anxious boy clinging to her side, and this strange man told them just to play and have fun while he was going to videotape them. They sat quietly, and pulled out a few toys, which Lenny cautiously and silently was willing to push back and forth. He picked up some beads and stared at them, manipulating them, rolling them between his fingers, trying to get himself grounded. This went on for a while, and when Mom left to talk to Tina, I got down on the floor to play with Lenny.

Up to now, he had not said a word. I lay on my stomach and with a little football in my hand inched toward him. "Oh, oh, oh, Oh, OH!", and then I moved toward his foot as if I would poke it with the football. He squealed. Again, I crawled forward. "Oh, oh, Oh, OH, OH!" He filled the room with his delighted squeals! We were able to go on like this, back and forth, me crawling toward him with a football, him squealing with delight for five minutes or so. I decided to throw a curve ball. I said, "I'm tired. I'm going to sleep." I lay down and started to snore.

"AHHHH!" he screamed, and pushed my shoulder with his hand, indicating that he did not want me to sleep and wanted the game to continue. I "woke up," and our game continued like this, my sleeping becoming more frequent, his squeals of laughter as I inched toward him, his insistence that we continue. I decided to make the game more complex.

I pointed to each of his feet with the football, but didn't approach. I asked, "Which one?" He paused. I paused. Finally, he lifted his right foot, ever so slightly. "Oh, this ONE!" I said with great enthusiasm. So, for a while, it continued like this. Squeals, me crawling, sleeping, pausing, him lifting his foot, until I decided to give it even more complexity.

He woke me, I crawled forward, and he held up his right foot for me to attack with the football. I said, "What?" I shrugged, my shoulders, hands up, gesturing my question, and waited. In the long pause that ensued, me standing like the statue of a confused quarterback, him staring at me, giving me no indication that he understood me, until finally, slowly, quietly, he lifted his foot and softly said, "More."

Like many parents, Lenny's Mom tells a story of "normal" development, interrupted by an event, often the MMR vaccination, that they feel changed his development, and the course of his life. "Lenny was developing right on time, he hit the stages, until the age of one. When he received the shot, the MMR shot, he went like into shock. He stopped doing everything. He didn't respond to his name. He couldn't hold anything in his hand, he stopped speaking, he started grinding his jaw, he became very sensitive to people touching his head, noise as well. He can't hear a parrot or he goes insane. He lost eye contact, he wouldn't respond when you called his name like he used to. I reported it to the doctor, but he told me to wait, that sometimes that happens, or maybe he's teething. But, I went outside and started looking for some answers, then I found out about early intervention. He was evaluated by them. They saw that he did have some delays. He was approved for those services at home. They came to the home and started working with him. It didn't go so well, because they had some personal issues. They would come to the house and one would have had a fight with her boyfriend, and one was getting a divorce, so he did not progress that well. The only one who really did well with him was the OT, because she was so excited working with him. When she walked though that door Lenny jumped really high. The way she came in, like she was so excited to see him. Should would call his name, 'Lenny!' I mean he paid so much attention to her, that he would progress far more with her." This phenomena, the high-affect teacher, in whatever method, getting much better results, has been well documented. You probably have that idea, or you wouldn't be reading this book, but kids develop in high-affect relationships. This is, after all, a book about kids in a DIR school!

"Then after he aged out from the early intervention, he went to another school that primarily uses ABA, he made tremendous progress, he learned how to read, he was toilet trained, he was able to start holding a cup, he was pointing at objects and saying the names, he was calling people by their names. Month to month you saw him progressing, pro-gressing, and I was like, 'Oh wow! He's coming back!' His next school was a public school, and the girls there really knew what they were doing, so he made progress. Then they moved him to another school; he didn't do too well. He started to have a lot of repetitive behaviors, he started to tantrum, he was six years old. He got no OT for the entire year, because they didn't have available time for him, so he just got worse. That whole year went wrong."

Mom went to get some training in Son-Rise, and began working with Lenny at home. She feels that it helped, but they told her not to approach her son when she was "stressed or down." She feels like it was good advice, but also felt like she was always "stressed or down," because she was just so distressed at the condition of her son. It was very difficult for her, but she "shook it off," and mustered her energy, and began working with her son at home. She began to see that she was getting better results with Lenny than they were at school, and so she really went at it.

"One day I used my older son, my middle son. 'Michael, I want you to ask me a question, and then I'm going to ask Lenny a question, and I'm going to see how he responds.' I said, 'Michael, ask me where I'm going.' "

"Where are you going?"
"To Dunkin' Donuts. Lenny, ask me where I'm going."
Lenny asked, "Where are you going?"
"Dunkin' Donuts."
To Mom's infinite delight he asked, "Well, why are you going to Dunkin' Donuts?"

"I thought, '*Well, okay!*' So I said, 'To get some coffee. Do you want anything?' "

"Nooooo." Mom laughs at the memory.

"That was the first time I ever heard him having a conversation, back and forth, like a loop. And, I was so excited that I took off from there. I started working with him more. When I approached him my behavior was different. I didn't say, 'Lenny you've got to come here!' I was like, 'Lenny, look what I've got here!' I was more creative with the way I approached him.

"There was this thing he used to do with his arm. He would look through his arm, he would look through his elbow." Mom brought the crook of her right elbow up to her eyes. "He had a thing where he would always do that, and put it over his eyes. So I started doing that, putting my elbow over my eyes, to see what he sees. And I finally saw it, you can see like a reflection, you know? I said, (she squeals with delight) 'Oh, I can see it!' He just looked at me like, 'What's wrong with you?! What are you getting so excited about?' My other children did it, and he never did it from that day on!"

So Mom, although she had never read about or seen DIR, came to us already with a beautiful, fluid understanding of having high affect, of working on circles of communication in a continuous flow, and of following her child's lead, even when it meant trying to understand a difficult stereotypic behavior and what he saw in it. This was a family ready to come to Rebecca School and fly with DIR.

Lenny started at Rebecca School in the first year, so that at this time he has been in the school for one-and-a-half years. However, he was home schooled for the first three months of his second year, due to a number of factors, and had to make the transition back to the Rebecca School program. Coming back was really tough for him. He screamed and cried for an hour before Mom was able to leave on the first day back, and then he cried for another hour, and it took him the rest of the day to recover. The teacher reports that transitions in general are difficult for him, and that if he is out of school for any reason, a holiday, an illness, a long weekend, the transition back into a long school day is difficult for him. Lenny has a hard time with scheduling changes. His teacher tells a story about this.

"Today, for instance we switched the Floortime session for the obstacle course. I said, 'It's time for obstacle course.'"

He said, "No, it's time for Floortime, I've got to have my Floortime!"

She continues. "When he's regulated, he is absolutely phenomenal; he practically Floortime's the staff! But, I feel like Lenny's anxiety is the major obstacle for him. Sometimes there are predictable incidents, like when Mom drops him off for school. A lot of times it's a reflection of his rigidity. Other times he is scared of certain things, like Mom mentioned, if a truck is coming down the street he may not want to come downstairs. He has a hard time with escalators; he doesn't want to go downstairs. Lenny's visual-spatial skills are really high, but his visual-motor skills are really low.[1] I think the sensory integration issues cause a huge, huge amount of anxiety for Lenny. Whether it is going from our classroom on the sixth floor to the lunchroom on the fifth floor, or when we are on a walk and we approach a curb and he cannot step down with one foot, he will have to jump down with two feet; his visual-motor processing difficulties cause him major anxiety. He can very quickly become dysregulated if he feels rushed, or if he feels insecure in his body and not confident about what's going to happen next. When he first came back, during one of the first gym sessions, there was a wedge-shaped mat, and Lenny would not, could not, lay on his side to roll down it. He cried and said he did not want to do it, and I told him he didn't even have to roll, that he just had to lay down and try it, so he physically removed himself from the situation."

The teacher gives another example of how Lenny's visual-motor system inhibits his functioning. "Every week, we go on a class trip to the grocery store, and it just so happens that there is an escalator to get down into the grocery store. The first time we went with Lenny, it took thirty-five minutes of trying to coax him gently to just walk up to the edge of the

---

1 The teacher is implying here that Lenny can see things perfectly well, and put together a logical plan to accomplish his goals, but cannot get his body to do the things it would have to do to put that plan into action.

escalator, touching it with his toe. And, he got up the courage to do that and I thought he was ready to go, and then he backed up very quickly, and he bumped into me. And, when he bumped into me he threw his hands in the air, and he collapsed to the ground and he started screaming, 'Don't touch me, don't touch me, don't, Don't, DON'T!' And he got so upset thinking that I was going to force him on, and probably so scared at his inability to picture what it would be like on the escalator (which is not scary or dangerous to most people) that it took forty-five minutes to calm him down. When he finally did it, he was so happy that he skipped right down the aisle. The next couple of times we went, it was a process, but he did it. The last couple of times he was not able to do it at all. He has gotten so upset at just the thought of trying to get on the escalator, that we just haven't had any success with it.

"When Lenny is regulated, and when he has himself under control, he is capable of the most amazing things. When he first came to school in December, he had a hard time initiating, even with adult support, with a peer. The kinds of interactions he had were pretty narrow, his vocabulary was limited, there were just a lot of constrictions in his abilities. Last week, Lenny was sitting on a beanbag chair in the corner, and a TA and a student were trying to open a bag of cookies. And the student was trying to open the cookies as hard as he could, and he was saying, 'Open the cookies, it's stuck, IT'S STUCK!' It was this very high-affect interaction that they were having, and they couldn't get it open, and the student said, 'Scissors, we need scissors!' The TA was Floortiming it, and said, 'Scissors. That's a great idea! I wonder where the scissors are?' Lenny got up from the beanbag chair, went and found the scissors, went over to his friend, shoved them toward him and says, 'Here Are Your SCISSORS!' "

"A TA and a student were going back and forth about a snack, should it be one cookie or two cookies. Lenny looked over, exasperated, and said, 'Make A DECISION!' "

In the time that Lenny has been back from his break where he was home, he has made tremendous progress. From the quiet, almost inert child whose fondest wish was to be alone with as much of himself in contact with the ground as possible, he has bloomed into an interested, attached, sometimes frightened, but brave young man, taking his first uncertain steps into new and exciting territory.

### Sensory and Motor Strengths and Challenges as Understood and Described by the Rebecca School Staff

*Visual Spatial:*

- Good visual-spatial awareness.
- Has a good sense of body awareness; does not bump into people or objects in his environment.
- With vision obstructed he can identify parts of his body being touched.
- Visual-spatial processing is a relative strength.

*Auditory:*

- Easily overstimulated auditorily.
- Auditory processing challenges, with improving receptive language.

*Proprioceptive:*

- Enjoys physical activity with proprioceptive input.
- Loves to roll across a floor on his own or in a barrel.

*Vestibular:*

- Enjoys swinging in a linear plane and prefers to lie on his stomach.
- He is fearful of a rapid descent down a ramp on a scooter.

*Tactile:*

- No longer has difficulty taking off his shoes and socks in the gym.
- Enjoys sitting in a bin of rice and beans.

- Recoils if something unexpected touches his face or body, for example when playing ball.

## Feeding:

- Has limited preferred foods, and has difficulty manipulating food in his mouth.

## Motor Processing and Planning:

Processing is a relative strength, but planning suffers due to his difficulties integrating visual-spatial processing and motor processing to create a plan, particularly if more than one step is involved. This leads to the very reluctant and anxious profile we see in Lenny, where a preferred strategy would be to lie still, connected to the floor in as many points as possible. Also contributing is his decreased body strength.

### Rebecca School Program in Place Before Consulting with Dr. Greenspan

*Floortime: 4–6 x 20 min./day, Individual, in the classroom, with teacher or one specific teaching assistant, primarily.*

Level I: To help Lenny stay regulated across demanding visual-motor tasks.

Level II: To help Lenny expand relatedness to peers.

Level III: To support his natural interest in other people's emotions, and perform in increasingly subtle social situations. To support him in a more fluid, continuous flow.

Level IV: Expand, his just-emerging problem-solving skills. Although Lenny is capable of higher developmental levels, focus must be on getting a continuous flow at Level III, and beginning problem solving at Level IV.

*Speech: 1 x 30 min./week, Individual, 1 x 30 min./week in a dyad, 1 x 60 min. in a specialized feeding group facilitated by a speech-language therapist and occupational therapist.*

- While Lenny is generally intelligible across contexts, he continues to speak with a somewhat limited range of motion of the lips, tongue, and jaw.

*OT: 2 x 30 min./week, Individual.*

- Therapy has focused on improving sensory-processing abilities, gross-motor coordination and control, visual-perceptual/visual-motor skill, bilateral integration skills, and attention/focus, as well as improving problem-solving skills and logical-thinking abilities.

*PT: 2 x 30 min./week, Individual.*

- Reciprocal stepping pattern, without handrail, for stairs, fluidity, increased stability.

*Music Therapy: 1 x 30 min./week.*

*Art Therapy: 2 x 20 min./week, with two peers.*

## Dr. Greenspan's Recommendations

Lenny, a young boy who is nine years old, has been attending the Rebecca School for two years, with a three-month interruption in the fall of his second year. He can be calm and regulated, but can become dysregulated when he is anxious, feels insecure about his body, when making transitions, and when he is frustrated. Two of his great strengths are his ability to engage with warmth, and his enjoyment of relationships with others. He can enter into two-way, purposeful communication and get into a continuous flow of back-and-forth interactions.

He can do shared, social problem solving in a continuous flow.

Lenny can use ideas and has lots of words and uses sentences. He can do pretend play, but tends to do it around reality-based themes rather than fantasy. He can connect ideas together and answer all the "W" questions, including "Why" questions.

In general, we want to expand Lenny's emotional range at all the levels as well as to expand the physical activities that he can do so he feels more secure. He has a good verbal memory and is able to be somewhat abstract in his thinking, but loses this ability when he is dysregulated. We want to get him to the higher levels of thinking

## Constitutional and Maturational Variations

Contributing to Lenny's challenges are difficulties in a number of processing areas. His visual-spatial processing is good in some areas, certainly he relies on close visual inspection of fine details, for instance. However, he does not see the big picture, does not see the forest for the trees, and he needs these skills to become a more abstract thinker. He has challenges in motor planning. These motor-planning issues stem from his problems with sequencing and his challenges in body awareness. His challenges in this area are also made worse by his mixed sensory reactivity, and his particular sensitivity to vestibular[2] sensations and his sensitivity to being in spatial configurations where he doesn't feel well grounded.

One of Lenny's real strengths in processing is his good verbal memory. We can use this strength to work with him, and lean on it to help strengthen areas where he has challenges.

---

2   Vestibular System: The sense, centered in your inner ear, of where you are in relation to gravity. Many of our children have difficulty with processing this system, and so have real trouble navigating through the world.

## Game Plan

The team at Rebecca School is doing a wonderful job with Lenny, as are his parents. Below are some suggestions to strengthen an already excellent program:

1. Have one or two key people do creative Floortime with Lenny three to four times a day. In the Floortime sessions with Lenny, thrown in curveballs and get him into areas where he is not as comfortable. This will help to expand his creative range and to see if his characters can be more elaborate in their feelings. This should be done very gradually over a period of time and if he becomes too anxious, help him come back to a theme that is more comfortable for him.
2. The school team and the parents should consult to determine what experiences are calming and soothing for Lenny to help him become re-grounded when he is dysregulated. These should not be experiences or things to distract him, but experiences like firm pressure or rhythmic activities, which may be very helpful for him.
3. In OT or PT, Lenny should do some balance exercises. Improving his cerebellar functioning will help with his vestibular system. The exercises can be standing on a balance beam or squishy pads and then closing eyes, standing on one leg, etc. Do this in a fun way and bring pretend themes into the exercise sessions.
4. Work on the vestibular movements starting very gradually, working up to where Lenny enjoys getting off the ground. Use materials where he can get onto elevated platforms, go up and down slides, swings, and where he can do it under his own control and talking about how he feels while he is doing it and experimenting with his body in space. This will help him be more secure with his body in space.
5. Keep working with all the motor-coordination exercises.
6. Do the *Thinking Goes to School* program, trying to get Lenny through the whole program rather than just bits and pieces. See where he runs into challenges. He may have trouble with some of the motor-based exercises but do better with the conceptual exercises.

7. Pair Lenny with kids who are interactive and verbal, even if they are a bit older, so that he has a chance to form some relationships. I recommend that the parents arrange play dates for Lenny on the weekend inviting kids over who are very verbal and interactive. Create games to get them started and then let them take over.

The key for Lenny now is flexibility, coping with emotions, progressing up to higher levels of thinking, and forming good relationships with peers.

### Program Response to Dr. Greenspan's Recommendations

Classroom: While very little time has passed since the Dr. Greenspan made suggestions for changes to Lenny's program, there have been changes, particularly in Lenny's general level of activity in the classroom. On the very next day after receiving the recommendations, his favorite TA, Ronnie, had him up in the air, above his head, coming down the hall. Lenny was flailing and complaining, and laughing, and the goal of getting him off the ground, with his feet not on the earth, was achieved. Since that time, Lenny has spent a lot of time spinning, flying, and generally moving in ways he had not previously. When I asked Ronnie what other changes had occurred since Dr. Greenspan made his recommendations, he said, "Basically, we're pissing Lenny off all day long!" Ronnie was joking, but was in essence telling me that the team took seriously the suggestion to continue to push Lenny to grow, and to throw him more curveballs, so that he can increase his flexibility. Other changes in the program are in progress.

## Chapter 5

# Looking Through a Shattered Lens

"What are we going to do with Helen!" The classroom teacher in our newly created beginning Floortime class looked at me incredulously, with her hands outstretched, in a gesture of supplication. Helen was the littlest, cutest sprite, dark hair pulled back, tiny, bright, and kinetic. On day one, she ate two shirts. Two of her own shirts, off her body, string by string. She unraveled them, and only constant physical intervention by a teacher or a TA stopped it for a second.

Despite this, Helen charmed everyone. She was bouncing from spot to spot, shifting her attention about every three seconds. It looked as if everything was a surprise to her. A look of shock, like she had suddenly encountered a wall in front of her as she bounced around, flashed across her face constantly. Then she would grab a string, pull it and eat it.

She had a picture book of family memories that she liked, and she would look at it briefly, then look up into the face of the adult nearest her and say, "Awww," as if she had found the family picture to be the cutest thing in the world, and she wanted to share this with you. She would put her hand on the side of her face, and tilt her head. This posture universally melted the heart of whomever she pointed it at, and people found her simply irresistible. Then, she would bounce away again, stop, look shocked, eat some shirt, then grab her book and be endearing. Two minutes with her was almost fatally exhausting.

As exhausting as it was for adults, it must have been triply exhausting for Helen. She seemed to only be seeing, hearing, and feeling in flashes.

Answering the classroom teacher's question about what we were going to do, I asked, "What do you think it's like for her to be in the classroom?" The teacher, one of the best DIR/Floortime practitioners on our staff, immediately recognized how disorienting being in the less-structured Floortime room must have been for Helen. I said that I had this vision of Piggy from *Lord of the Flies*, with fractured glasses, feeling paralyzed and vulnerable as he looked out at a splintered world. For me, it seemed like Helen was only seeing, experiencing the world in flashes. I told the teacher that for Helen, it must be like being thrown from a plane, at night, in a thunderstorm, your world only illuminated by unpredictable flashes of lightning, unable to feel where you are in relation to gravity, tumbling in the flashing darkness. The string eating and the cute, "*Awww,*" all provided temporary moments of clarity, signposts in her chaotic, unpredictable world.

Helen's mom described an easy pregnancy and birth, after fertility treatments. "It took us a long time to get pregnant with Helen. She was a quiet child up until about seven months, at which time she got a lung infection, and went into the hospital. She was there for about two-and-a-half weeks, and while there they realized that she had some deficits. She wasn't developing as quickly, she wasn't sitting up, so they hooked her up with EI. We started OT and PT at that point. She was in EI (Early Intervention) through the age of three, and she moved to CPSE[1] at that point, where she went to another school. She was there for two years: the first year in a more-structured ABA type of program, the second year in a less-structured program. After she aged out of CPSE she went to a CSE at another school.

"When she started with EI they quickly realized she needed more than she was getting. So, within a few months they started feeding therapy, and then speech. So she had a full day very early in her life. I was reading

---

1   CPSE: Committee on Preschool Special Education. If a child continues to need special services after Early Intervention, or is identified for the first time as needing services after the age of Early Intervention, the CPSE system takes effect. EI is for toddlers through age three; CPSE is for ages three to five.

a book, *Let Me Hear Your Voice*, and I learned about ABA. So I inquired about that, because that sounded like something that would be helpful to Helen, and I found out that she could have ABA. So the first real introduction for us as far as seeing progression in Helen, was at that point ABA.

"The first ABA therapist walked in the door, and I guess Helen was about three years old, and she wasn't really speaking, she said, 'Mama, Dada, and baba,' at that point.

"She walked in the door, stuck Helen in a swing, pushed the swing for about fifteen minutes and said the word, 'Push. Push.' To the point where I thought I was going to die. Then she stopped and said to Helen, 'Helen, what do you want?' and Helen said, 'Pu.' And I said, 'Wha?' and she said, 'Helen, what do you want.' And Helen said, 'Pu.' So at that point, good or bad, I was hooked on the idea of ABA. So Helen's first entry into school was in a very structured ABA program, which went very well. She started to blossom, to the point where they decided to put her into a less-structured type of classroom, where she started to regress. At that point the kids in the class were very social, a lot more advanced than she was; she wasn't speaking. So, we started seeing some regression.

"Jumping ahead a little bit, we figured that ABA was the key to Helen's future, and we found out about another school, and put her in that school, without really knowing enough about it. So her last year was a very, very difficult year, because ABA at the new school was not what she had been getting. What she had been getting at home was repetition, reinforcement, and fun. ABA at the school was discrete trials[2] over and over and over. She hated it, and she became very angry and very frustrated. She was a very frustrated little kid by the end of the year.

"Medically, she had a year when she was eight months to around eighteen months when she was seeing various doctors a couple times a month for this one infection that mysteriously showed up and then mysteriously would go away."

---

2   Discrete trials: A particularly strict form of Applied Behavior Analysis.

Dad interjects, "At first they thought it was reflux, then they thought it was gastroenteritis; they just didn't know. And, it turned out to be nothing."

Mom continues, "But during that year we did all of the sleep studies, and the PET[3] scans and the MRIs[4] and pretty much jumped through every hoop—we were committed, and we wanted to do it. And, we kept hearing that everything was fine. Everything was always fine. And, we just wanted to hear one test to say, 'It could be . . .' But, it wasn't.

"Other than that, she's been a healthy kid. We've done all of the tests, and the nutritionists, and the homeopathies, and the cranial-sacral; we've done all that stuff. But, health-wise, she's fine. We started her on medication in January, maybe a year-and-a-half ago. Basically, when she took her neurological test to get into kindergarten, when she went in for the test, the woman who was doing the test said, 'I can't test this kid!' She was just all over the place. And she came back and said, 'I just want to make a suggestion, would you consider medication?' I remember at that time that I had thought of it, and I thought that Helen's dad had probably thought of it, but we had just never said the words out loud. Because we figured that somebody would have probably said, 'Have you considered . . .' if it was really valid. And, we certainly didn't want to go down that route if it would lead someplace we shouldn't be. But we said, 'Sure.' So she started on Focalin[5]. A very, very, very low dose of Focalin. And within two weeks her teachers were saying, 'This is not the same kid. You know, she's sitting at the table, she's doing her work.' So of course, like the nuts that we are, if a little is good, more is better. So, they gave her more Focalin, they upped it. And it went the opposite. She had horrible diapers, horrible stomach, throwing up, it was just bad. We kind of went through a lot of medications since then, Adderall[6], Strattera[7], Risperidone and now she's

---

3    PET: Positron Emission Tomography. A medical imaging technology capable of showing activity in live tissue, and giving three-dimensional maps.
4    MRI: Magnetic Resonance Imaging. A medical imaging technology used to look at detailed internal structures.
5    Focalin: To combat attention symptoms.
6    Adderall: To combat attention symptoms.
7    Strattera: To combat attention symptoms.

on something called Seroquel. And it's a very, very low dose, but what the aim is, is to just take off the edge. Helen sometimes feels like she is racing in her own body, and it's really hard to watch. So the whole aim, and that's what the Focalin did, was just to calm her down, enough to have a conversation, to look at her. And right now, we're not there yet with the Seroquel. We just changed it three weeks ago, and we have a psychiatrist who starts very, very low. He's conservative, and we take it slowly, so she doesn't have these negative reactions. She's had a lot of weight gain. It's hard, Helen was a little scrawny thing most of her life, under the fifth percentile. And right now she's gained a lot of weight since starting the Risperidone. We're trying to figure out the right doses now because she has gained five to seven pounds, which is a lot on her little frame. Right now we're playing with it a little bit."

"The Helen we had before June is not the Helen we have now (this was October). Before June, she was a much calmer, easy to interact with. Right now she is back to racing in her body. We can see it and we can feel it. We have a four-year-old boy and a three-month-old. And, the house can be very calm, and then Helen can come into it and you just feel the level go up, because she just goes from one thing to the next, and she does perseverate. Which is a huge issue, because I've spent most of my life praying she would say, 'Mama,' and now I just want to say, 'Shush!' And I'm sure anyone who is on the first floor knows that. She literally, I think we drove to Connecticut once and over one-hundred times she said, 'Mama, Dada, Mama, Dada. De, De, De.' Constantly. I just want to say, 'Calm.' And, there's no amount of hugs and compressions and stuff, it's just when she gets going it just keeps going. So it's been a highly stressful few months, with just her inability to calm down.

"The Risperidone we started because one night she came down when our baby was first born, she must have been very tired because she had that calm, and she sat on the couch, and she crossed her feet, and said, 'Hi.' And, we said, 'Hi.' It must have been like nine o'clock, because we were feeding the baby. And, it was such a level of calm, that we just kept looking at each other and saying, 'Do you see this?' And her

PECS book was out on the table. And she went down and she picked up the juice pec (PECS icon) and said, 'Ju.' And, I said, 'Do you want the juice?' and she said, 'S, peas.' So we went and got the juice, and she sat back on the sofa, and she was a joy. And, then I said, 'Do you want to go to sleep?' And, she got the 'I don't want to' pec and held it up. I said, 'You don't want to go to bed yet.' And, she said, 'O.' So we let her sit there, and I think I was feeding the baby, and she went and got the 'nap' pec. I said, 'Do you want to go to bed now?' And she said, 'S.' So I said, 'Go ahead.' And she went straight up the stairs and went to bed. We said, 'I don't want a drugged child, but that was the best interaction in months, it was just that calm. We talked to Helen for the first time in a lot of months. So we talked to the doctors and said, 'We've got to do something different, because there has to be a way of bringing her down, and still allowing that connection.'"

## Sensory and Motor Strengths and Challenges as Understood and Described by the Rebecca School Staff

### Visual Spatial:

- Tremendous problems in the area of visual-spatial processing.
- Has difficulty planning a path through an obstacle-filled environment.
- Very easily visually distracted.
- Often seems surprised by objects or people who appear in her visual field.

### Auditory:

- Easily overstimulated.
- Processing challenges, with improving receptive language.

### Proprioceptive:

- Responds well to deep pressure.

## Vestibular:

- Does not appear to seek vestibular feedback particularly.
- Will jump on a trampoline, but cannot jump forward due to poor visual-spatial abilities, and poor motor planning.

## Tactile:

- Does not present with any particular tactile defensiveness.

## Oral Motor:

- Presents with an open-mouth posture and poor control of the movement of her lips, tongue, and jaw, which impacts her speech production.
- Oral-sensory system is underreactive, as she constantly mouths string and fabric.
- Shreds clothing with her cuspids and runs the string through her mouth and/or chews on it.

## Motor Processing and Planning:

- Has difficulty planning a course through an obstacle-filled environment.

### Rebecca School Program in Place Before Consulting with Dr. Greenspan

*Floortime: 4–6 x 20 min./day, Individual, in the classroom, with teacher or one specific teaching assistant, primarily.*

*Speech: 1 x 30 min./week, Individual, 1 x 30 min. in a dyad, 1 x 60 min. in a specialized feeding group facilitated by a trained speech-language therapist and occupational therapist.*

- In order to provide oral input on a regular basis, her oral sensory motor protocol will include chewing on a chewy tube using her left and right molars, intra- and extra-oral vibratory massage, and the presentation of alerting flavors (i.e., lemon and peppermint) on a toothette. Helen has been slowly working toward tolerating this protocol by allowing vibration on her extremities and holding the chewy tube.

### OT: 2 x 30 min./week, Individual.

- Deep-pressure input in the form of a neoprene vest has greatly decreased the mouthing and shredding at school. Sessions to focus on improving sensory processing and finding appropriate self-regulation strategies to increase shared attention and engagement, particularly in small groups and with peers, as well as increasing motor planning and sequencing for improved participation in fine- and gross-motor tasks.

### PT: 2 x 30 min./week, Individual.

- Physical therapy will focus on:

Improving her overall muscle strength (specifically trunk musculature) and endurance to allow her to participate in community walks while staying regulated in the environment.

Improving Helen's ability to modulate her movements and increase her body awareness through improving her graded muscle control as she displays difficulty using the appropriate amount of force to perform a specific task, such as tapping someone to get their attention and sustaining that attention with something she's interested in.

Improving ball skills (throwing, kicking, and catching).

Increasing the amount and frequency of environmental and visual-spatial obstacles.

### Music Therapy: 1 x 30 min./week.

### Art Therapy: 2 x 20 min./week, with one peer.

## Dr. Greenspan's Recommendations

Helen is almost seven years old and has a history of GI challenges, and language, motor, and social interaction challenges. She had been in an ABA program for a while, and showed some positive gains there. However, Helen became frustrated by some of the repetition. Helen has been attending the Rebecca School since September and seems to enjoy the school and everyone enjoys Helen. She is popular among the staff and vice versa. Helen is currently taking Seroquel and building up the dosage. She initially had a good response to Focalin, but then when the dosage got higher, Helen began having some negative responses.

Helen can focus and attend, but is very easily distractible. She can be so distractible, mostly visually, that it is hard for her to maintain her focus and she can become dysregulated and shred her clothing. She is easily overstimulated visually, and then goes into an action mode and becomes hyperactive and jumps from one thing to another. When this happens, it's a little hard to settle her down. I'm sure one of the goals of the Seroquel is to help her settle down more easily.

She is very popular, is "the mayor," and always seeking engagement. I'd like to see the staff at the Rebecca School help her develop more intimacy, with one or two staff persons being the main ones to work with her. We shouldn't be matching her frenetic pace by jumping around too much from person to person. She can be purposeful and get a continuous flow of back-and-forth interaction going, but this is more difficult for her when she becomes distracted. However, high affect usually keeps her engaged and interactive, but in our discussion there is a fragmented quality to the engagement, rather than a problem-solving quality.

Helen has a little more difficulty stringing together many circles of communication to solve a problem, especially when she becomes distracted, and depending on her mood. However, she has ideas and you can get lots of exchanges with short phrases and single words. During these exchanges she can answer some of the simple "W" questions, like

"Where" and "Who," but is not yet able to do causal thinking and answer "Why" questions.

Helen needs work to strengthen Milestone IV and expand Milestone V. This may be most easily accomplished by doing more pretending with her. Then, staff could move more solidly into Milestone VI where she could answer "Why" questions and you could have a long conversation with her. These goals are very much within her capacities, because she is a bright little girl and her receptive language is stronger than her expressive language.

### Constitutional and Maturational Variations

Helen has challenges in auditory and language processing. Her greatest challenge is in the expressive language area, with the receptive being a little stronger. Because she has motor-planning and sequencing challenges, she can become fragmented very easily. She is overreactive to visual stimuli, but is also very sensory seeking and can get hyperkinetic. Instead of shutting down or becoming more cautious, she goes into the action mode and seeks out more sensation. To help with this, Helen's visual-spatial processing needs more work, because she tends to get lost in the details rather than see the larger goal in front of her.

### Game Plan

Helen's strength of engagement and receptive understanding make her prognosis good for continued progress. The overall program for Helen seems excellent, both at home and school. There are a few things I suggest adding to her program to help her progress a little further. First, Helen should have a two key staff people assigned as primary contacts for her: one in the morning and one in the afternoon, or taking turns every hour-and-a-half, or so—whatever works best. These should be people she really likes and who like her. Second, do more pretending with Helen and challenge her to use more imagination to build up her capacity to use ideas in a more regulated way. We want her to use that considerable intelligence she has to express herself.

My third suggestion is an important one, having to do with Helen's challenges in modulation. When Helen is somewhat regulated, in all your interactions with her, look for opportunities to do fast, slow, and super-slow. Match her to pull her in and then slow down, go up and then slow down again and then slow down more so that you are giving her lots of opportunity for regulating and going up and down the scale of action with her. You could be playing the drums with her, moving or swinging, or other activities that lend themselves to slowing down or speeding up. When she is dysregulated, counterbalance her by being very soothing and comforting. Try not to hype her up further by letting her get you frenetic. We want to help her settle down at those times rather than speed up.

My fourth suggestion is a referral to some outside experts. Helen may be a good candidate for seeing a developmental optometrist. He or she may have some ideas and suggestions that may help regarding her visual sensitivities. A nutritional consultation may also help. Eliminate any foods from Helen's diet that are stimulating, like sugars and processed carbohydrates. Have her on foods that are very calming.

Finally, in reference to the Floortime you are doing with her, don't try to do too many different things at the same time with Helen; slow things down. Everything should be calming and methodical. Helen should do a lot of balance exercises, like standing on cushions on one leg; walking on a balance beam; throwing and catching a ball while standing on the beam. She should also do lots of obstacle course and treasure hunt games, things that will call on all levels of her processing, with emphasis on her visual-spatial processing. At home, do a lot of Floortime with Helen with pretend and imaginative play and long conversations: Mother should try to do at least two thirty-minute sessions, and Dad at least two thirty-minute sessions. Overall, we need to help Helen have longer conversations, we need to always counterbalance her mood, and to not match her frenetic pace.

## Rebecca School's Response to Dr. Greenspan's Recommendations

The classroom took one, calm, quiet, observant TA and made her Helen's one-on-one. This TA, Elizabeth, became Helen's constant companion, and Helen's beloved "E." Over the course of the rest of the school year, Elizabeth took her peaceful intervention to Helen, and Helen calmed down and became less fragmented. Elizabeth's entire intervention is based on respect; respect in all its meanings, as outlined by Elizabeth in a presentation she did for the school at the beginning of the new school year, in her new role as a member of the Floortime team:

> The word "respect" means to pay attention, to be dutiful, to show consideration, to avoid intruding upon and violating. We gain the respect of children and show our respect for children by how we behave with and around them.
>
> How do we give and gain respect? There are many active ways to demonstrate our respect for children in our care. The following are a few examples of respectful and disrespectful behaviors.
>
> Educators, therapists, parents and other adults show respect for children when we:

- Allow children to be intentional.
- Allow children to make choices.
- Ask the child's permission to enter their space. For example, asking a child before wiping his or her nose.
- Allow and encourage their developmental levels.
- Allow transition time from one activity to another.
- Avoid setting up power plays over food, toilet, etc.
- Give flexibility, affection, respect, and moments of undivided attention.
- Give clear and reasonable limits with opportunities for negotiations.
- Give respect and attention.
- Have patience and a sense of humor.
- Set limits with guidance.

Educators, therapists, parents and other adults are disrespectful to children when we:

- Use angry words under stress and, in particular, direct angry words toward children.
- Finish children's tasks for them, rather than giving encouragement or directions allowing them time to finish tasks for themselves.
- Answer questions for them.
- Shout or use sarcasm.
- Rush them.
- Do not take care of our own physical or emotional needs.

Respect is shown when children get recognition for who they are and what they do, when they are allowed to exercise options and make choices within acceptable frameworks, and when their choices are acknowledged and accepted. It is too easy to disrespect children because they are physically small, are more dependent than most adults, and have less ability than do adults to control their needs and wants. They need more explanations, they need more time and their behaviors are childish because they are children, not yet capable of conforming to adult standards.

In the warm glow of this respect, and the consistent calm presence of "E," Helen has become a more focused, smiling, winning child who is beginning to ask questions, and respond in ways other than putting her hand on the side of her face, saying "*Awww*" and tilting her head in an endearing way. She knows other people are there, sees things more clearly, and is not in a state of constant surprise. She has begun to piece together a more intact world, through a no-longer-shattered lens.

Chapter 6

# Punt, Pass, and React

I was walking down the street with Tina, the program director, when I felt something whizz past my head, and bounce off a large brown delivery truck with a loud "*THUMP!*"

"What was that!?" I looked around as a football bounced back past me. I ran over and picked it up, as it rolled to a stop after rebounding off the California Pizza Kitchen on the sidewalk next to us. "Tina, I think this football came off our roof!"

"No, it couldn't have!" She shook her head in disbelief.

Our rooftop playground is thirteen stories up, and overlooks Thirtieth Street where we were standing. The building department has regulations for rooftop spaces in a school, which should come as no surprise. There is a ten-foot fence on top of a three-foot wall, with a three-foot return angled at forty-five degrees back toward the space. It is a formidable barrier. Childproof by design.

Tina continued. "If there is a child in this school that can punt, pass, or kick that ball off the roof he shouldn't be here, he should be in the NFL!"

So meet Rock, youngest player for the New York Giants, all of seven years old, and ready to lead his team to victory, and able to defeat a fencing system designed by all the best minds, to stop footballs from hitting pedestrians thirteen floors below.

Rock is a beautiful boy, big eyes and beautiful braided hair. He carries himself with the easy demeanor of a child comfortable in his physical abilities, and truthfully, he surpasses most of his peers, and his teachers as well, in the physical realm. I cannot help but think of him in the future, captain of his school's football team, cheerleaders, and admirers around him, lifting him on their shoulders after a spectacular win. Or, I see him as the homecoming king, presiding over his court. He has that kind of charisma and ability. But those days are in the future, only if we do our jobs here, and to that end we have worked hard to understand Rock and the places where his developmental and processing profiles have left him vulnerable.

Mom spoke to us about Rock in the week after being burned out of their home. They had not been able to return to their home after the fire, but they were eager to tell their story. Mom started, "When Rock was six months he started to say, 'Dada,' and he had a couple of words. He was standing in his crib. And then at eight months, he just totally stopped speaking, he was very withdrawn, and by ten months we knew that something was wrong. We decided to get him evaluated. I was in denial. I said it was only speech, but they told me it was speech, PT, OT, and I thought it was only speech. He did get EI services in the home for about two years. He had a special educator in the home. Then when he went to preschool he started getting services in increments. He got speech; he got OT then PT. When he received PT he started to talk. That was like, 'Wow!' to us. That was at about three years old."

Dad interjects, "We realized that he was not in the right program at three, because they did not have the right services, the early intervention program. So we decided we had to get him all the services that we could."

Mom continues. "Rock was in three different schools, two different boroughs, and that was before pre-K. That's all before kindergarten. Once he got to kindergarten we knew we had to find a place, so he was sent to a special-education school. We thought it was good, but the principal was not supportive at all. He didn't want to deal with the services, even though it was a special-education school. He kicked Rock out of the school, and then Rock was out of school for months.

Dad says, "So they had an emergency IEP (individual education plan) brought in, and they gave us what they had at the time, and that was a problem for him because it was three different schools in one building. That was just too much for him, it was just too overwhelming."

Mom continues, "It was a public program, and OT was next to the lunch room, which had a capacity of about 400 kids, so it just didn't work. And then he ran away from school, he hit staff, he had temper tantrums; there were a lot of problems. So, they recommended medication for him. We did it, we tried it, we didn't like it. He was on Adderall, 20mgs of Adderall. The positive side of the meds is that he could sit down, he didn't have those tics and shakes, and he was able to take in a lot of academics. It did help him with the academics. On the other side, because he was already a picky eater, he wasn't eating, and his sleep was dysregulated. He didn't sleep. While he was on Adderall, he pulled two full-grown teeth out of his mouth. The dentist couldn't understand. Then we decided we wanted to go to Rebecca School. That was last summer. Once Rock came to Rebecca School, we decided, 'No more meds!' We wanted to start fresh, and we really wanted to implement the Floortime model to help him. We didn't want him to be dependent on medication, because he's a good kid. He loves sports; he's a sports fanatic. He loves the museums, he loves video games, he loves to travel."

The parents describe with admiration the loving boy that they know, and recognize that he needs help with some things that are holding him back.

Describing what he needs is another matter. He is very attentive, very attuned to what his classmates are doing. He processes input from the outside quickly, in contrast to most of his peers who have processing delays. He also turns information around quickly, so that he puts a motor plan into action almost immediately. This skill will serve him on the sports field, so long as a long-term plan or deep understanding is not needed. For instance, no long-term plan is needed as a linebacker zeros in on you to flatten you; what is needed is some instantaneous effective action. However, where Rock falls down is when he has to take an ambiguous or a long-term course of action that requires abstraction. In other words, if he has to imagine a unique plan to avoid some future linebacker, he cannot do it effectively or reliably. So, in the absence of an immediate, present situation, requiring some facile motor plan, he feels at a loss. He has real strengths at some of the higher FEDMs, but he is "Swiss cheesy" at the lower levels, an expression we use at Rebecca School to indicate the FEDMs at the lower levels being full of holes. Without real solidity at the lower levels, these higher levels topple over and become ineffective. He lives in the realm of the reactive "now," and this is an uncomfortable place to be.

One way to control your anxiety around being in the reactive "now," the land where the linebacker is bearing down on you to smear you, is to be the "actor." This is what Rock chooses to do. He will see an opening, a chance to grab a desired toy, run to a desired spot, or escape a situation, and he will be off in a flash. Since we tend to gravitate to situations that have emotional meaning for us, Rock creates high-affect situations with his actions. It is difficult to create loving, warm, emotionally charged situations with lightning-quick physical actions that come upon the other person with no warning. Try it. At best, you will fail. At worst, with the wrong person, you will get arrested! So, Rock often finds himself using his quick physical system to provoke his slower processing peers: for instance, grabbing something from another's hand before the other can even react. By the time his friend realizes what has happened, Rock is running away, laughing. He looks like the aggressor, but really, without lower levels being solid, and without a firm grasp on the more abstract world, what other choice does he have if he is going to create emotionally meaningful interactions?

Rock, by virtue of his quick physical processing is a "leader" in the classroom by the teacher's description. Once he sees what is expected in a given situation, he is the first to carry it out, but he is not always the first to understand what his required. I watched a recent science lesson in Rock's class, and as expected, Rock took the lead. But if you watched closely, you could see that Rock really didn't have the concept that was being taught, but by watching others he could see what physical action was going to work to solve the problem. He had a block of ice with arctic animals frozen in it, and the teacher wanted to encourage students to solve how to get the animals out. Students puzzled for a while, they had different melting techniques at their disposal, but Rock only watched the other students for clues as to what was being required. He didn't really understand that the goal was to free the animals. Once he realized that was the goal, and that the teacher was letting you pick your method, he jumped up from the table, got a toy hammer, and began whacking away at his ice block. It was ineffective, as the ice was too hard and the hammer was too soft, but he persisted. Other students used rock salt or table salt, or heat, but these techniques held no appeal for Rock. Finally, as the other students began to have success, Rock grabbed some salt, and continued with his hammer. The combination worked, and after Rock freed his animals, he began to go after the other students' ice. He whacked away, they often did not get their fingers out of the way, and he "helped" them free the frozen animals. Finally, he got less interested, and began to run around the room. With most teachers and the rest of the students still focusing on the lesson, he began to rev up, and you could see that he was looking for a way to initiate an interaction. Finally, he poked a friend who could not resist the provocation, and the class quickly degenerated into a wild chase, tug-of-war, wrestling match. All of this happened so quickly that the teachers barely had time to react, and so found themselves having to break up the resulting tumult.

### Sensory and Motor Strengths and Challenges as Understood and Described by the Rebecca School Staff

*Visual Spatial:*

- Good visual-spatial awareness. This is a particular strength.
- Has a good sense of body awareness; can navigate quite easily through his environment.

## Auditory:

- Continues to display difficulty with auditory processing as he is unable to consistently follow complex, multistep directions in a group setting.
- With moderate scaffolding cues, Rock is now able to maintain a logical, related conversation for four to six conversational turns.
- Rock's ability to answer "W" questions continues to be a challenge. While Rock will respond to all "W" questions, he continues to confuse his responses (e.g., "Who should get the game?"— "on the table.")
- Rock has made significant progress grouping pictures and objects into concrete categories (e.g., animals, vehicles) however, he continues to demonstrate difficulties with more abstract category groups (e.g., things that are sharp).

## Proprioceptive:

- Enjoys physical activity with proprioceptive input.
- Loves to jump, run, and crash into people and objects.

## Vestibular:

- Seeks movement constantly.

## Tactile:

- No challenges noted.

## Oral Motor:

- No challenges noted.

## Motor Processing and Planning:

- Rock is able to coordinate two movements together such as running up and kicking a ball, however displays difficulty when the movements he has to coordinate involve both his upper and lower extremities such as jumping jacks.

- He is able to achieve the two separate body positions, however displays a tendency to keep his legs shoulder-width apart when the task is sped up.
- He is able to skip with alternating feet for fifty feet, however has a tendency to stop and restart when the pattern becomes out of sync.

### Rebecca School Program in Place Before Consulting with Dr. Greenspan

*Floortime: 4–6 x 20 min./week, Individual, in the classroom, with teacher teaching assistant, primarily.*

- Level I: Can stay regulated. Proprioceptive and vestibular input help.
- Level II: Has difficulty attending consistently due to receptive language-processing difficulties. Visual cues help.
- Level III: Can get his needs met, often by himself, but has difficulty maintaining an emotionally meaningful, co-regulated interaction with another.
- Level IV: Will problem solve by himself, but needs considerable support to problems solve around any situation where the solution is not readily apparent, or supplied in a multiple choice way by the other participant in the interaction.
- Level V: Will play imaginary scenarios, of his own creation, if physical play is involved. Often these involve fixed play, where the subject has a demand. For instance, he will run the bases and hit the ball if an imaginary baseball game is involved, but will not offer unique or unusual variations not specifically called for by the play at hand.
- Level VI: Only very early skills at this level.

*Speech: 2 x 30 min./week, Individual, 2 x 30min./week, in a group.*

*PT: 1 x 30 min./week, Individual.*

*Art Therapy: 2 x 20 min./week, with two peers.*

## Dr. Greenspan's Recommendations

Rock is eight-and-a-half years old, and has been attending the Rebecca School since July 2007. He has a history of having had developmental challenges dating back to the end of the first year of life. He is doing well and making lovely progress at the Rebecca School, holding nice conversations and the staff is all working well with him. Since being at the Rebecca School, Mom says he is engaging and learning how to regulate himself.

For the most part, Rock can be calm, regulated, and attentive. However, at times he can become dysregulated when overloaded. He is very engaged, sweet, and likable.

He can enter into two-way, purposeful communication and do this in a continuous flow. We want to increase his flexibility to deal with wider range of emotions, including transition, disappointment, and not getting his way. Rock can do shared, social problem solving, can be creative, and do a little bit of pretend play. He can answer "W" questions, but has a hard time with "Why" questions.

## Constitutional and Maturational Variations

Contributing to Rock's challenges are difficulties in a number of processing areas. He has auditory-processing and language challenges, and motor-planning and sequencing challenges, but is improving in this area. In terms of sensory modulation, Rock can get overloaded and sensitive, and this can lead to him being a little impulsive and sensory craving. Visually, Rock has visual-spatial challenges, which leads to him being able to see the trees clearly, but not the forest.

## Game Plan

Everyone at the Rebecca School is working well with Rock. Here are a few suggestions to strengthen his current program. Do six twenty-minute, one-on-one Floortime session each day, working on increasing Rock's creativity and imaginative thinking. Spend a lot more time in pretend play activities, having Rock make up stories and playing with action figures to get him to higher levels of logical thinking. He is a good candidate for the *Thinking Goes to School* program. He's a bright youngster who is engaged and can hold a conversation and these exercises will help him become a big-picture thinker.

We want to help Rock tolerate a wider range of emotions and to have words to describe when he is upset or doesn't want to make a transition. We also want to help him do that when he is getting dysregulated. Very gradually introduce more challenging situations for Rock at school. These could be done just a tiny bit at a time so that he becomes more comfortable with disappointment, frustration, annoyance, etc. In terms of academics, we want to work on Rock's capacities to think things through. Nothing should be memory based—all should be thinking based. When you do multiple choice with Rock, give him a good choice first, and a silly choice second. This will help him to think. All of these goals require more one-on-one interaction with Rock, which is critical for him to move forward.

### *Alla Sheynkin, MS, Ed. at the Rebecca School offers the following about Rock*

Rock is the type of child that can lead us in the wrong direction when we are trying to create an appropriate program for him. He has so many talents, presenting with strengths in language and motor planning, effectively distracting us, and masking his challenges. The key to Rock's success is for us to not concentrate on his higher skills, which of course is so tempting, but instead to spend a lot of the time working on his lower FEDMs. In order to help Rock with his impulsivity and inability to slow down and stay in longer interactions, we need to get him into long chains of back-and-forth interactions, focusing on silly games filled with anticipation and warmth. For example, if he really likes tickles or lotion, a teacher or a therapist can sit with him and engage in a high-affect game of reaching for his foot or arm at snail's pace, moving slowly enough for

Rock to be able to predict where the tickling or lotioned finger will reach him. Rock has the tools to become the football team captain or the home-coming king, or anything else that he desires to become, but he doesn't know how to use those tools just yet. Playing in the above described way with Rock for twenty minutes, although seemingly childish, will be tremendously helpful; it will give him the key to opening the toolbox, allowing him to fill the Swiss cheese holes in his early development.

## Chapter 7

# Yes, I Have Dimple

Sometimes, when kids come in for admission to the school, instead of Floortime, I have to do "Hang Out Time." It's really just Floortime for the older, more verbal crowd. When Joanne walked through the door, with a book and a shawl, I knew I wasn't in for a time of watching her and her Mom interact around the Elmo phone, or a run around the big open space we were seeing other kids in then. It really wasn't hard to know that this young girl reading a big, hardcover chapter book as she walked in, was not going to toss a ball with me, or anyone else for that matter.

Her mother made it very clear that she did not interact with Joanne around toys of any kind. My typical request to have the parents just have fun playing with their child was not going to fly with this family. I told the mother that she could spend the time with the program director, and I would spend some time with Joanne. Joanne folded her knees under her and bent all the way over at the waist with her book in front of her. She looked like a religious devotee, praying in the proper geographical direction, prostrate to her deity. In this case though, the worshiper was bowing in respect to her book. I tried to ask her what she was reading, but had no success. She picked at her skin constantly. She asked me, "What is a female pig who hasn't had a litter called?"

*Now, I'm in for it,* I thought. "I'm not sure. Why do you ask?"

"Because," she said, "A female pig who has had a litter is called a sow. So what is a female pig who hasn't had a litter called?"

"Well, I don't know. Was that in the book you're reading? Maybe you can tell me a little about the book."

"I can't read this part."

I went over to the book. "Oh, they're speaking French here. *Très amusant* means 'very amusing.' Did she say something clever or amusing up here?" I touched the book and pointed to it. We found the place in the paragraph above where the heroine was amusing, and we were off. Joanne began to speak, but she spoke with the voice of the characters in the book, as she imagined them. She was deeply immersed in the book, and did not seem to particularly care whether what she was repeating was complete or made sense, and certainly not whether what she was saying related to me or what I was saying. While she was very charming and entertaining, she was not with me. The exception was when I was answering questions about things that had confused her in the book. I noticed that the main character in the book was named Jo Ann. I asked her, "Are you like the Jo Ann in the book?"

"No, we're not alike at all. We're not even spelled the same. She spells her name without an 'e.' "

"And you spell your name . . ."

"I spell it with an 'e.' "

"Is the girl your age?"

"No, not even close. She's seven."

"How old are you?"

"I'm twelve; not even close!"

Later, she started talking about her mosquito bites. "We only get bitten by the females. The males don't eat blood."

"No, they drink from plants, they stick their sharp noses (knowing what I know now about Joanne, I would have said 'proboscices') into plants. I guess if we were plants we would hate male mosquitoes more than females."

She looked at me with her head slightly cocked, and pondered. Then, I think she decided that I was smart enough, and interested in things like she was, and therefore, I was okay with her. From then on, for half an hour, she rattled on across a wide range of subjects that interested her. Finally, in reference to something that someone had said in her book, she asked me, "If someone asks you if you have dimples, and you have only one dimple, what do you answer?"

And, for one of the first times, but certainly not the last, Joanne had me stumped. I said, "I don't know."

The beginning of school was terrible for Joanne. She was on the young end of the oldest classroom in the first year at Rebecca School, and when the school opened most of the forty new students had come from schools or home schooling that were more structured to say the least. She was frightened. She was a very intelligent, but fragile and concerned twelve-year-old, who suddenly became aggressive and violent. This lovely, charming, bright young girl, when she did not feel supported and safe, fragmented and became furious. We immediately did everything we could to change the situation, but Joanne took a long time before she trusted us again, as she had the first day.

"The thing that was interesting about Joanne, even when she was two, was she was interested in books." Mom begins to talk about Joanne's developmental history. "She was absorbed in books, and when we would read to her, even before she was two, she would take our hands and point to the words. She really wanted me to be giving her visual cues. Her language development looked normal to us. No cause for concern." Dad interjects, "One of the earliest things we noted, we thought it was just a funny thing, she referred to herself as 'You.' We would ask, 'Are you thirsty,' and she said, 'Yes, you are thirsty.' We thought it was kind of a funny thing. She also had issues with cadence." Mom picks up, "She had a singy-songy voice. When she would play with toys, she would act out a scene from a TV show. And, it would have to be verbatim. And, if I tried to introduce a little variation, like the lion would say this instead of that, she'd get very upset, and start all over again. One time she was in a play group, and there were lots of other two-year-olds in the group. She really didn't interact with the other two-year-olds, she would sit in the corner with a book, or just kind of play with things by herself. I remember that someone was really impressed when she stood up and said, 'Excellent, excellent, extraordinary,' and she kind of said it in the right context, but it was a thing she had picked up, a piece of language from a television show. We just thought she was incredibly precocious; we didn't really know what to think.

"She did not know how to interact with other kids. In preschool, she would walk up behind a kid and hug them, and she really had no idea if they were okay with it or if they were trying to pull away. Even with grown-ups, she would try to interact and not get these cues from them." Dad jumps in, "She always had a blanket. Even now, when she goes to bed, she likes to have the blanket wrapped around her. You know, what I would think of as an itchy wool blanket, she wants to have it wrapped around her, a sensory thing."

The preschool she was in picked up on all of her social problems. She was in a program that really emphasized the social deficits, and they began to speak to the parents about her. She became violent, hitting other children and tantruming. They told the parents that she had a sensory integration problem and recommended OT to them, which they got, along with a SEIT. The SEIT really acted as a facilitator between Joanne and other kids. Dad says, "I got her a Calvin and Hobbs book, and she saw this one comic she really liked. Calvin was having a dream, and he dreamed he was going to a robot doctor, and he had the top of his head sawed open, and more brains were stuffed in so that he wouldn't have to go to school anymore. Well, she just loved this. So she was on a play date, and she said to the other child, 'We're going to play Calvin and Hobbs, and I am going to saw off the top of your head and stuff more brains in.' Well, obviously, the other kid was not too enamored of that idea, she just didn't get it at all. But, that was Joanne." Mom continues, "She couldn't answer questions about how someone might feel or why they would do something. If you asked her about how Laura might have felt when she left the little house in the big woods, you could see her scrolling through her head, and if it said it in the book she could answer. But, if not, then she couldn't."

Joanne has OCD[1] - her symptoms have gotten better and worse, then better, then worse again over the years. She has seen behavioral therapists

---

1  OCD: Obsessive-Compulsive Disorder is an anxiety disorder in which people have unwanted and repeated thoughts, feelings, ideas, sensations (obsessions), or behaviors that make them feel driven to do something (compulsions).

and that seems to help. The introduction of Ritalin made her OCD worse again; another round of therapy and Strattera seemed to help. Then, "At the end of fourth grade, Mom went back to work again, full-time. Basically, that would be me. And, basically, she started to get upset and got much, much worse at the end of fourth grade. She was running into the street, and just stopping, because basically she was upset about something. And so then we switched the medication stuff around. We tried Seroquel, we tried Focalin[2], but that made the OCD worse than it's ever been. She was picking up mounds of garbage that she was carrying around with her. He (the psychiatrist) took her off the Focalin, and it didn't really go away. That's when we tried Seroquel because she was running into the street and doing dangerous things. Seroquel was just a bad, bad drug for her. She wasn't quite as aggressive, but she was still aggressive sometimes, and she still had OCD, and she was a complete zombie. She had a terrible year in fifth grade. We got a big name child study center in there to try to help her from a behavioral approach. I'm not sure how effective that was, and by the end of fifth grade we changed her meds again, to Risperdal, that seemed to help a little, and then she came to Rebecca School.

"Her best back and forth: She and I recently just read the latest Harry Potter book," Dad says, "and we were talking about which of the characters' deaths were the most difficult for her to take, to absorb. Which ones was she most upset about, least upset about, things like that. She said that Dobby dying was the most upsetting for her. And I asked her why, and she said that it was because she had read in another book that Dobby was most likely to live, and that if he could die then who else might die. And when I said that what she was worried about was not Dobby dying but that others would die, she wanted to be sure that I understood that she was also sad for Dobby. She did not like me saying that." Mom says, "At her worst, if the conversation at the table doesn't include the six things

---

2   Focalin: Focalin (dexmethylphenidate) is a mild stimulant to the central nervous system. This medication is a modified version of Ritalin (a common medication for attention disorders) and contains only the most active component. Focalin is used to treat attention deficit hyperactivity disorder.

she knows a lot about, she'll just begin talking about the six things she knows about, as opposed to joining the conversation."

The classroom sees many of the things that the parents reported in terms of her interests and intelligence. She continues to seek out staff and adults instead of peers, although lately she has begun to interact more with the boys in the class. Two of the boys in the school have crushes on her, and while she does not encourage them, she clearly enjoys their attention. She loses interest if the conversation is not rapid enough or intellectually stimulating. The teacher says he is working on high school-level algebra, functions, graphing points, and ordered pairs. She can do virtually any computation in her head, rapidly. In relation to her progress through the more complex levels of interpersonal thinking, including gray-area thinking, a TA offers, "We were in gym, and she didn't want to participate, and she said she didn't want to participate, and I said, 'Well, how upset are you? Are you more upset by this, or by when you missed art.' And she said, 'Nothing is worse than missing art.' So I said, 'Then it's not so bad, then?' And she said, "No, but it is still causing me never-ending agony!" Another TA offers, "What is evident here is that when she is dysregulated she really isn't able to do any of the gray-area thinking or reflective thinking, but when she is regulated and calms down, then she is able to find that in herself."

Building a trusting relationship with Joanne is key. She remembers if someone has lied to her or made a promise and then followed through. Another TA adds, "Gym was never her favorite subject, and Joanne could explain that she felt clumsy and wasn't good at it. 'Some people are good at sports, and others are book-smart,' she would say. So she would often refuse to participate and read her book from the sideline. One time she dropped her own book and a page ripped out. She bolted out of the gym, laid on the bathroom floor and hysterically cried over the separated page. I followed her and asked if the book could be repaired, which of course it could, but Joanne could not have visualized that possibility on her own in that dysregulated state. Once she calmed down a little, knowing that my relationship with her was strong enough, I carefully and coyly pointed out to Joanne that it looks like she may have overreacted a bit. I gave her an overexaggerated example of an instance that might deserve such a reaction. She laughed a little and calmed down. I jokingly called her a drama queen; she was able to laugh at herself. Then we fixed her book together and she went back to the gym."

### Sensory and Motor Strengths and Challenges as Understood and Described by the Rebecca School Staff

**Visual Spatial:**

- Good visual acuity.
- Cannot put together her entire visual field to make sense of the world; cannot see the forest for the trees.

**Auditory:**

- No sensitivities noted.

**Proprioceptive:**

- Seeks deep pressure that appears to calm her.
- Seeks full body contact for support, so will lay in a beanbag chair whenever available.

**Vestibular:**

- No sensitivities noted.

**Tactile:**

- Has difficulty standing close to other people.
- Does not like to be bumped.
- Picks at scabs, and does not appear to feel it.

**Feeding:**

- She stuffs her food.

**Motor Processing and Planning:**

- Difficulties with motor planning, related to visual-spatial difficulties.

**Integration:**

- Difficulty integrating sensory information.

### Rebecca School Program in Place Before Consulting with Dr. Greenspan

*Floortime: 4 x 20 min./day, Individual, primarily with classroom staff.*

*Speech: 2 x 30 min./week, Individual.*

*OT: 2 x 30 min./week, Individual.*

- *Thinking Goes to School* 1 x 20 min./day, with classroom staff.
- 1 x 30 min./day in the sensory gym with class.
- Class does activities from *Thinking Goes to School* and *Brain Gym*, daily.

*Music Therapy: 1 x 30 min./week.*

*Art Therapy: 2 x 30 min./week, with two peers.*

### Dr. Greenspan's Recommendations

Joanne is twelve-and-a-half years old and comes with a history of having been diagnosed with Asperger's or high-functioning ASD. She has always been characterized by both her phenomenal memory and having islands of cognitive skills that are more advanced than her years, yet has difficulty with putting all the pieces together, holding a conversation, having peer relationships, and has trouble with internal regulation. She can focus and attend when motivated. She can engage with others and everyone likes her very much. She can do two-way communication in a continuous flow, and shared, social problem solving also in a continuous flow. She is very creative with her use of ideas. She creates stories and can be very imaginative with what she reads.

Joanne can connect ideas together and can answer all the "W" questions, including "Why" questions. She can do some advanced thinking, like giving you many reasons for why she likes something, do some comparative thinking, and has little islands of gray-area thinking. Joanne is not quite at the reflective thinking level. Joanne can also be very polarized in her thinking and when she is dysregulated can get impulsive, give up ideas, and use behavior discharge. This was her pattern when she was younger, but has been improving. Joanne can also use avoidance as a coping strategy when she is overloaded.

We see that for each of these capacities where Joanne has some islands of skill, she lacks the stability, depth, and flexibility to use them fully. Therefore, the key at all these levels is to improve the range, depth, stability, and flexibility of these capacities so they are no longer islands, but present all the time in all situations. The best way to think about Joanne is that while she is making progress, there is too much fragmentation in her capacities.

### Constitutional and Maturational Variations

Contributing to Joanne's challenges are difficulties in many processing areas. She clearly has strength in her verbal capacities, but she still has challenges in using her language for the full range of human emotion and intensity and abstract thinking. Joanne has big challenges in perceptual motor, motor planning and sequencing, and body awareness. She can get quite overloaded with other children near her and with touch. She can also get a little sensory craving when she gets impulsive and lashes out.

Joanne has instability in her mood and gets overloaded, impulsive, and can go into the action mode.

If we do a full evaluation of Joanne's visual-spatial thinking, we will see some strong visual-memory skills, but also enormous challenges in her ability to use visual-spatial thinking to feel comfortable in space and to understand her relationship to her world which contributes to her anxiety, getting overloaded, and being emotionally very reactive.

## Game Plan

The fact that Joanne is doing so well at the Rebecca School and at home and has been making such good progress is a very good sign. Joanne is an emotionally very sensitive girl and always has been. Even though she is on medication and has been given a diagnosis of high-functioning ASD that usually leads us to think about the biological components and the use of just medication, biology and environment and experience are not isolated from one another. Sometimes your biology makes you even more sensitive to your environment and, for example, can make someone looking at you in the wrong way more upsetting than for a person who doesn't have this sensitivity. Due to Joanne's sensitivities, she lives in the "trees" and will overreact to subtle things in her environment.

Here are the elements that I recommend adding on to optimize her already wonderful program. Joanne needs very solid, long-term, key relationships with people who are very nurturing to help her put the pieces together in a solid way. At school, the people who are identified as her primary nurturers should spend at least two hours a day in creative, imaginative Floortime-type dialogues, where she is creating stories and being expressive, always following her lead and natural interests. When she withdraws or becomes avoidant, try to change the rhythm and draw her back in. A mental health person should be working closely with these key people to help her use those solid relationships to cope with her emotions, and not use avoidance or all-or-nothing thinking.

At home, Mom and Dad should spend as much time as possible with Joanne, where Mom especially is as close and nurturing as possible. Basically, follow the Floortime philosophy in this "hang-out" time, following her lead, being creative. Have lots of long conversations with her following her natural interests, whatever they are. Don't be intrusive or demanding, but be empathetic and nurturing. Dad should do the same as much as possible. It is very important to create this nurturing atmosphere for Joanne.

To help improve Joanne's visual-spatial thinking, she should have a very strong visual-spatial program at school. She should be doing the exercises in the *Thinking Goes to School* book for two twenty-minute sessions every day. She should also have a strong program to help her with body awareness and perceptual motor skills. This program should be done three or four times each day for at least twenty minutes each session. She is also a very good candidate for doing lots of drama and working with music and rhythmic activities, all of which will be helpful for her.

The big goal is to help her experience the emotional glue that will help her put all the pieces together so she is not experiencing the world in a fragmented way, gearing up her processing capacities, and developing strong nurturing relationships at school and home. This should help Joanne make even more progress.

# Chapter 8

# roarrrr!

If a strong wind came up suddenly, or if you got caught off guard with a sneeze, little Martin might just blow away, or so you might feel when you meet him. He is slight, and fair, and there is a translucence that suggests frailty, although he is not frail. He is a boy, in a class full of boys, and he bumps and bruises along with the biggest and most aggressive of them despite his slight stature. He is quiet, mostly, although he makes his presence known with startlingly loud, piercing squeals. He is ethereal in appearance, but stay with him for five minutes, and you get the sense of a rugged individual waiting to find his voice.

The teachers describe him as yummy, and adore this affectionate five-year-old boy who loves to kiss them. When I first met him, a year-and-a-half ago, he was sitting comfortably in the cradle formed by his loving parents as he placed animals in a dollhouse. He softly named them as he put them in, "Cow, Doggy, Cat, Meow." It was clear that this boy felt safe and secure with his parents, and had spent much time on the floor with them. I said, "What would happen if you animated the kitty?" Dad, jumped in. Mom followed.

"I'm the Daddy lion!" Dad roared.

"And I'm the Mommy lion," Mom gently purred. "And this is Martin," she said as she took a little cub and placed it gently into Martin's lap. Daddy lion crawled up Martin's arm and kissed him.

All of this, the play fantasy of Mommy and Daddy and the Cub Martin went on for a while, and it seems to me in retrospect that much of it may not have had much meaning for Martin. But still, Martin changed, and became more smiley while they played with him. He looked up and away from the little plastic play pieces that he had previously been scrutinizing so carefully as he labeled them, and looked into his parents' faces. He was laughing. When they would slip into naming things again, I gently prompted them to play, and then sat back and watched as these three enjoyed each other, and Martin basked in his mother and father's love and connection with him.

"My husband and I were a part of the television program about Martin's birth, and for anyone who sees that, they say it was an emergency C-section. It was not." Mom laughed with the easy confidence of someone who has been in front of audiences for much of her life, which in fact she has. She and her husband are actors. "That was the Hollywood version of his birth. It was a C-section because he was too big. I had a dream pregnancy, no complications, everything was perfect. Developmentally, he never crawled, he never rolled over. I spoke to my pediatrician several times, at length, and when he hit his first birthday I started asking questions about why he didn't crawl, why he didn't roll over, and I got a lot of answers like, 'Einstein didn't speak until he was six, and he's going to do what he wants to do when he's ready to do it.' But there was one significant event that made me change pediatricians. I had gotten so used to, Martin was maybe ten months old, I was so used to, I could leave him on the edge of something and walk away because he didn't move. And when I took him in to be examined at the table and the doctor walked away, and I took Martin's shirt off and started to walk away, and the doctor turned around and leapt at the table like, 'What are you doing you crazy woman!' I never thought, because this was completely normal for me, because he didn't move.

"He never was much of a babbler as a baby, and not very smiley. But, if we tapped on his hands it would get him to laugh. We would tickle his hands. At about eighteen months old he I was sitting next to the bathtub and trying to get him to say the word 'baby.' I had a little picture of a baby on his shampoo or something, and eventually he did. Day after day we would do this. He would say 'bay' quite clearly, and then he added 'be' and he would do both parts if I prompted him both times. We have cats, so he started saying 'meow' when he saw the cats. By the time he was two, those were gone. He would not say them anymore. I think he maybe said the 'baby' together one or two times; that was it. I mentioned all of these things to my pediatrician, and he said, 'He'll talk when he's ready,' and all that kind of thing. So we switched pediatricians.

"My new pediatrician observed him for about five minutes and said, 'It's not Autism because he is looking at me, but have you heard of the early intervention program, because that will help with his speech?' She got us started with the early intervention program. He was doing an ABA program five days a week, two-and-a-half hours a day. He also got OT two times thirty minutes a week, and speech therapy two times thirty minutes a week. We hated the ABA, and so did Martin. We used to call them 'the vampires that came to our house.' Because they would come through the door, we had several different people, for the most part the people who worked with him were very nice, but Martin would see them and run away. Just to see him seated at a table for hour after hour when he was two-and-a-half, making him tap the table and touch his head, and making him do ridiculous things that didn't seem to be doing anything. We stuck to it until he aged out at age three, but we had pretty much had it by the end of that, and so had Martin. We felt like his little soul was being kind of extinguished. He had gotten smiley and a little more interactive, and that seemed to be going away. He started parroting things they would say during the day. I would ask him anything, like, 'Do you want something to eat?' And he would say, 'Hi, Mickey,' because that was his therapist's name, and that's what he had to say eight times a day in order for them to check it off. Around that time we got the opportunity to go on the road and do a show for a year. If we thought the therapy was even working, if we thought we had other options, we would never have even considered it. We just wanted to get him away from these people, who just wanted to point out what was wrong with him, and what he wasn't doing, and how many times he hadn't done something in a day. We asked all the people he was working with, including the pediatrician, and they all seemed to think it could be great, that you could never tell what was going to bring language with children. Maybe a yearlong vacation with your parents isn't such a bad idea. So we went.

"It was around that time that I first read about Floortime. I remember something clicking in my brain, that we were doing Floortime before we knew what it was. I was involved in every single one of Martin's sessions from twenty-seven months old to thirty-six months old. My husband was involved when he could be as well. I literally sat in on every hour of everything he had. Because I'm an actress, I'm a good mimic, so I could mimic what they were doing with him, but rather than have him sit at the table I just started working with him while he was standing at the sink, playing with little animals, running water, something like that. I tried to elicit language, and a connection and engagement with him that way. We went on the road, and we were unofficial, full-time, Floortime therapists. It was certainly not a wasted year. I sometimes second-guess myself; I wonder if we had found a place like Rebecca School how much farther along he would be. But, you know, you can drive yourself crazy with that. He did gain ground during the year, and we did see improvements. Just the things like, we were moving, sometimes on a weekly basis, sometimes we would stay in place for four or five weeks, but being in a new environment with new people with constant stimulation, might have made him completely shut down. But he didn't. He thrived in that environment. He seemed to really enjoy it."

Martin has been at the Rebecca School since he was four-and-a-half years old, and he is now six. During that year-and-a-half, the parents have seen lots of change. "This was the first classroom setting he had ever been a part of, the first school setting, and he loved it. He immediately took to it and started thriving. He learned the names of his peers and spoke fondly of them at home. Even when he just lists their names, you can see that he has a great deal of affection for school, and for his peers and the team here. As recently as last summer to have a conversation with Martin I would say, 'Do you want something to eat?' And he may or may not have answered that. Then I would say, 'Do you want this, do you want this, do you want this, do you want this?' Then he might repeat the last thing I said, or he might repeat one of them. Then I would say, 'So you want a sandwich,' and he would say, 'Yes, okay.' And that was a big deal, because we had a little give-and-take, we had some kind of reply from him, and some sort of engagement. Now he can open and close circles, I stopped counting." When Martin is regulated and interested, he is able to go back and forth with his mother for a long time, and to her, this is a miracle.

His speech is more purposeful now. Mom tells a story about this. "A significant difference in his speech is that he struggles now. Before he would say to me, 'I want yellow.' And I would say, 'What's yellow?' And he would just look at me with this dejected look on his face and he would repeat, 'I want yellow.' Or he might just walk away, like 'You didn't get it; I'm not going to try anymore." Now, we had this exchange.

He said, "I want yellow."
I said, "What is yellow?"
"I want this yellow girl."
"What is this yellow girl?"

"This yellow girl, this hair, in the tubby." Because we had this doll that has wild hair in the tub the week before, and he remembered that. So the fact that he can put those things together, and let me know and didn't give up, and that he wanted to struggle. He is so proud of himself at times like that, when he sees that he has communicated something to us. That's really amazing."

On the subject of Martin's relationship with other students, Mom says, "The other day he was out riding his bike, and his friend, Eric, who has just turned four, was riding a big wheel. Eric said, 'Let's race!' He wanted to ride around the back and have Martin follow him. Martin did not quite get the concept of racing, so I said, 'Let's get Eric.' So we were going in one big circle and stopping, and we'd go in one big circle and stop. So Martin got off his bike, and I thought, 'Well, that's it.' But then he went over to the big wheel, and put his hands on the handlebars, and said, 'Martin's turn!' So I said, 'Maybe Eric can ride your bike. So we switched. So Martin liked being on the big wheel, and he would look back to see if Eric was chasing him, and we went back and forth over that for a long time."

The family does a lot of things together, often sitting at a table, playing. Mom points out that Martin does spend a certain amount of time independently. "He likes to be on the computer. The computer is very centrally located, so he is never by himself on the computer. That is where he will be if I am home alone with him, and I need to do something in the kitchen. He's always sharing with us when he is on the computer. He is constantly saying 'ma'; he is constantly telling us something that is happening. One of his longest utterances came from the computer. He said, 'Mama, the rabbit, she eating the pink spoon.' He turns around and wants me to clap for him and he says, "I did it." Things like that. He does love the computer. We have to turn the computer off sometimes, because he would stay on it forever. We have seen some imaginative play. Lately he has been feeding a doll, and he likes to blow its nose, and he seems to have come up with this himself. He has this phonics computer toy that he plays with that has been really amazing. It's got all the alphabet and it can teach you three-letter words. There are several settings where it just tells you things, and settings where you have to push the right buttons to get a response. It's so amazing that he can now do that. He will sit and listen to that and it will say, 'F-O-X spells fox. What are the letters that spell fox?' And then he will search for the letters. Then there is a little place where you have to write it, and you can do it in small case or large case. And that has been something he has been taking a significant amount of time at home to do. Again, he is never more than two feet away from us, if not on top of us, because he wants to share with us."

Martin makes a variety of high-pitched squeals that Mom describes this way. "Screaming, slash, squealing, slash, a sound like a dog yipping. It makes us crazy; it makes us crazy! He has always done some vocalizing, that type of thing if he is watching something, like the Wiggles or something. If they are singing he will be squealing at the top of his lungs, trying to match the pitch or something. The singing and the squealing had gotten sort of to crisis proportions, and I am hoping it was because of this flu he has had. It was when he was understimulated, when he was over-stimulated, when we were on the subway, just random. And he would just let out these yips, these loud squeals, these screams. We've tried ignoring it, we've tried punitive things, 'Go in your room,' we've tried, 'We don't do that,' we've tried taking things away, we've tried very calmly taking his face in our hands and saying, 'We're not going to make that noise anymore.' We can't find any pattern why he does it, or when he does it, or what will make him stop. But that is our number one challenge right now.

### Sensory and Motor Strengths and Challenges as Understood and Described by the Rebecca School Staff

*Visual Spatial:*

- Easily distracted.
- Visual-spatial processing is a relative strength.

*Auditory:*

- Easily overstimulated.
- Auditory-processing challenges, with improving receptive language.

*Proprioceptive:*

- With input can attend with minimal support.
- Uses a weighted blanket for deep pressure.

*Vestibular:*

- No differences noted.

*Tactile:*

- Can stay engaged with input, such as rice and beans, shaving cream, accordion pipe, bumpy toys, vibration on his limbs, or massage.

*Feeding:*

- No difficulties noted.

*Motor Processing and Planning:*

- This is a relative strength.

### Rebecca School Program in Place Before Consulting with Dr. Greenspan

*Floortime: 4–6 x 20 min./day, Individual, in the classroom, with teacher or one specific teaching assistant, primarily.*

- Focus on Level I, to help Martin to stay regulated, and Level II, as Martin has difficulty remaining engaged without direct adult support.

*Speech: 3 x 30 min./week, Individual, 1 x 30 min. group.*

- To address moderate delays in expressive, receptive, and pragmatic language and auditory processing. Therapist gets fifteen to twenty circles of communication in individual sessions, which she attributes to small, quiet space in which she sees him.

*OT: 3 x 30 min./week, Individual, 1 x 30 min, in a fine-motor dyad with another child.*

- Most sessions take place in the sensory gym to help him regulate his sensory system to support his communication. He is given time to calm himself at the end of the session before he returns to the classroom.

*Music Therapy: 1 x 30 min./week.*

- Shares attention, regulates, is beginning to be able to get into a continuous flow.

***Art Therapy: 2 x 20 min./week, with two peers.***

- Focus on peer interactions, with adult support. Help to tolerate frustration, and to regulate even when frustrated. To support interactions, circles of communication, in a continuous flow.

## Dr. Greenspan's Recommendations

Martin has been attending the Rebecca School since Jan 2007. He has a history of having language and social delays—he had language when he was a toddler but then lost it. Initially, Martin had some ABA work, but the parents took him on a trip and did Floortime in a natural way during that time and he really thrived. Since Martin has been attending Rebecca School he has been making continued, lovely progress.

Martin can be calm and focused, particularly when he is interested in something. He can be well regulated most of the time, but when he is overloaded he can get frustrated and do intrusive and physical things to other people. He is fairly easy to regulate. Martin can be engaged and warm. When he is in a good, calm, soothing environment he can be engaged, sweet, loveable, and interactive. We want to deepen and ripen that by keeping the environment calm and interesting for him.

Martin can interact and be purposeful and do many circles in a row. He seems to be ready to get into the continuous flow if we keep him interested and not too structured. He has a lot of spontaneity and zest. He can do shared, social problem solving and combine many circles together. I think he is ready to move into the continuous flow by following his interests, not frustrating and overwhelming him but challenging him.

Martin can use ideas and has lots of use of words. He has been broadening his use of ideas and interactions and is showing meaningful use of language. He is doing a little bit of pretend play like feeding the dolls, etc. He is connecting ideas together, answering most of the "W" questions, but not yet "Why" questions. He is at the causal level, even though he is not answering "Why" questions verbally yet.

We do hear a little difference between what happens in the class-room, in one-on-one speech, etc., and what Martin does at home. In the classroom, Martin doesn't connect ideas together well, from what is said, but is doing so in one-on-one work in the therapy sessions. In a busy environment with lots going on Martin doesn't seem to function as well.

### Constitutional and Maturational Variations

Martin has challenges in auditory processing and language, but he has made some gains in this area since going to Rebecca School. He has relative strengths in motor planning and sequencing that we can build on. He can get overloaded easily, but he has some mixed elements to his sensory modulation. This mix means that we need to find his strengths in his ability to modulate, and build on these. His visual-spatial processing is a relative strength, but we want to work more with him to make this area even better.

### Game Plan

Martin has shown very good gains over the past year or so and we seem to be on a good trajectory for continued gains. However, I sense that Martin's world is a little too busy. What Martin needs is a soothing, relaxed atmosphere. The staff should be in a situation where they aren't overstimulated and that will help Martin be more calm and relaxed. This should occur at home, as well. However, when Martin is tuning you out, use high energy to draw him back in.

Martin should have at least six sessions of one-on-one Floortime each day with one or two people being the primary facilitators. Two people sharing this is fine, but they should compare notes and coordinate their work. The main thing is that we have to keep Martin's environment calm and soothing. The classroom is good because of the access to other children and access to a social group, but I think it is overloading him as he goes through the day. I recommend that the Floortime be done with Martin in a separate room, or in a separated area of the classroom if he prefers to stay in the classroom. We should try both and see where we get more imaginative pretend play and language. Work on the imaginative play and getting the continuous flow with a lot of pretending and language that accompanies this.

Regarding Martin's screeching, when he is dysregulated or beginning to do things that seem maladaptive or out of the ordinary for him, always assume that he is being overloaded in one way or another. This can be due to an illness, medication, a change in cleaning products or the emotional atmosphere at home. The remedy is to be more soothing and relaxed. Be less demanding, but just as interactive. For example, he can be director of the foot massage you are giving him (harder, softer, here and not there, etc.). At school, this means we want to be more soothing and also very gentle, but set firm limits when he intrudes physically with other kids or adults. First calm him down, soothe him, and then give him a time out or other appropriate limit-setting time. During the time out, talk to Martin about what happened. Do the same thing at home.

Martin is a good candidate for the visual-spatial exercises from *Thinking Goes to School*. For now, he should do these exercises for fifteen minutes a day, then increase the time up to two twenty-minute sessions a day when he is at the "Why" level. At school, he should be paired up with other students to do very interactive joint activities. At home, he should have at least two play dates during the week, with another child who is very verbal and interactive. Create a game for the children where they have to cooperate.

To get Martin to the "Why" level, because I think he is already capable of comprehending that, when he shows a real interest in something throw in a "Why" question and give him two choices—good one first, and silly one second. I believe he is capable of answering appropriately quickly.

Martin should have no chemicals, sugars, additives, or dyes in his diet. He should have complex carbohydrates (chewy fruits and vegetables, no fruit juices) and lots of protein. Try the gluten/casein-free diet to see if it may help, but I wouldn't make a battle out of it. Also, try to get Martin away from the jelly and bread because they both convert to sugar quickly. However, I wouldn't make this a central issue.

At home, the parents should do a couple of Floortime sessions in the evening, just interacting with him and following his lead and interests. On the weekends, do more Floortime and have more peer play dates. When Martin is showing any symptom like screeching, be more soothing and calming. The key overall point is a soothing, relaxing environment; building into his day a lot more regulating and soothing sensory activities; Floortime in an individual room or a segmented part of the classroom, but in a relaxed way where the person is not distracted.

### Program Response to Dr. Greenspan's Recommendations

Classroom: The classroom was split into two sections, four children in Martin's section, five children in the original classroom for large parts of the day, partially to support Martin's need for a less visually and auditorially stimulating environment. Martin has been able to increase the number of circles in a continuous flow within the classroom now, partially as a result of the less-stimulating class, and partially because the classroom staff have concentrated more on a continuous back and forth with him. As a result, they now see up to thirty circles of communication between them and Martin, something that only the speech therapist previously reported. Martin has also been reaching out more to his friends in the class, and will play with them, but this still needs adult support for it to be sustained. They continue trying to deepen and enrich his back-and-forth emotional communication, so that he can be in relationship to others across happiness, sadness, anger, and the full range of emotions. Martin will now begin to play a little in the fantasy world, and he is really enjoying dressing up and playing in the class's firefighter, police, and chef's outfits.

**OT: 3 x 30 min./week, Individual, 1 x 30 min./week in a fine-motor dyad with eight other children.**

- Martin now participates in a two- to three-step obstacle course, with a goal of using his relative strength in his visual-spatial system and using that to help him engage in problem solving, at the same time helping him stay in a continuous flow with the therapist. He will even seek out peers now to help him problem solve with the course. He also has begun to be involved in gross-motor games with his friends, sometimes playing catch and with, or mirroring them. As a result, he has made gains in handwriting readiness and bilateral coordination skills. He is more flexible with new activities in the sensory gym.

**Speech: 3 x 30 min./week, Individual, 1 x 30 min./week, Group, 1 x 30 min./week.**

- Martin has become more flexible in his play, able to choose new toys and activities during sessions. His struggles with verbal problem solving continue, and as he enters the realm of ideas, and wants to make his ideas known, he becomes frustrated. His screaming, or squealing, continues, but the speech therapist tries to help him more effectively communicate his exploding ideas.

*Chapter 9*

# Mischief Personified

"$H$e has such a good sense of humor. He just thinks everything is funny. For the last two months, he falls on the floor when he sees me, covers his face, and laughs." Alla, his translator, and the person who has developed the best relationship with him, talks with love and affection for this bright little boy with the devilish grin and mischief-filled eyes. She tells story after story about him. "Last week, we were in the Floortime room. He likes to run around a lot, so I don't chase him anymore. Eventually, he plopped himself down in a chair opposite me. I started calling his name, 'Oleg. Oleg.' He giggled in his chair and smiled slyly at me. So I did it again.

"'Oleg. Oleg.'"

He giggled. "*Kakashki*," (the Russian word for "poop"!) he said, and laughed. He curled up again in the chair, and hid his face.

"I said, 'Oleg. Oleg.' He laughed. This back and forth of giggling and shying away went on for many minutes. Finally, he jumped up, came over to me, and hugged me, pulled back, looked into my face, and giggled again. We went on to do some play on the floor, but his shy funny approach is what I really love about him."

Another time, one of his classmates was having a difficult day. He had defecated and urinated on the floor of the classroom, and had deliberately spilled Oleg's drink. Alla continues, "Oleg was jumping up and down when I came into the classroom. He ran to me and urgently said in Russian, 'It poops; it pees; it spills!' He was trying to warn me about the dangers of the other student!"

"One day he was being really difficult, scratching me, trying to hit me, just generally cranky and mean. I said to him, 'Why are you being so mean to me?'"

He looked me in the eye, held my face in his two hands, and struggled out in English, "You bother me!"

An encounter with Oleg is always memorable, whether he is running around destroying a classroom, like a tiny Harpo Marx, throwing things over his shoulder as he keeps one step ahead of his pursuers, or whether he is showing the real empathy he feels when he tries to stop another student from hurting himself. An encounter with him may be frustrating, but you always walk away very aware of the intensely vibrating life you have met in him. He challenges and amazes, and he has been a daily lesson in humility and joy.

Mom's primary language is Russian, and she speaks with some hesitancy in English, although her English is quite good. "I had a normal pregnancy with Oleg, and delivery was completely normal. He was born in Arizona, United States. When he was one-month-old, we returned to my native country, Russia, and my mother-in-law took care of Oleg. He was a very happy normal child. He made all his developmental milestones on time, except for his speech. Oleg began to speak one word at a time when he was nine months old, but he didn't begin to use phrases. That was a concern for me, but the pediatricians, even in my country, said that each child develops individually, so we waited for him to speak more.

"When Oleg was three years old we emigrated to the United States. I started to see that Oleg was more aggressive, and he lacked social skills with children his age. He started to go to daycare, then a second daycare, and he started to hit other children. That was a big concern for our family. We went to the pediatrician and the neurologist. Almost every doctor agreed that Oleg had some speech delay, but in other aspects he was normal. When Oleg was over three years old, the neurologist said that he had some autistic features. We did not know about early intervention, or any other interventions that were available for developmentally disabled children, so we hired a private speech therapist. We went to private Reggio Emilia school. He was taught one-to-one by the Reggio Emilia teacher.

"He is now eight years old. He underwent several big therapies. One big therapy was an Auditory Integration program in Provo, Utah. The result of this therapy was that he regressed, especially in the area of his memory. He was very good in memorization, not just visual, but auditory memorization and tactile. He would remember the name of the letter after touching sandpaper, but after this program, he lost his skills. Since that time, he has not recovered from the results of that program.

"Then we started to look for biomedical intervention. Even in Reggio Emilia school, academically he could count to two hundred, he started to read in Russian when he was less than four years old, but his social skills were less than a normal one-year-old child. We went to a treatment center that specialized in behavioral treatment for children and adults, especially for Autism and schizophrenia.

"Since then we are trying biomedical interventions including the anti-yeast program and B-12 injections. We started chelation[1] therapy because Oleg showed a very very large quantity of lead, mercury, and arsenic. We started chelation therapy in May, very recently. Also, Oleg underwent hyperbaric oxygen therapy in North Carolina. He went for three months, for more than a hundred treatments of hyperbaric oxygen therapy. It was very good for him because he became much less aggressive, his social skills improved. Plus, his digestive tract and his physical appearance became like a normal child."

Oleg had terrible experiences in the school he was in prior to the Rebecca School. Mom reports that the only words he learned in that school were, "Don't," and "Stop," so they had to convince him that it would be all right to come to a new school. "Since September, coming to the Rebecca School, even on Saturday and Sunday he asks me to come to the school, and he loves to come to the school. He has had a very positive

---

1    Chelation: Chelation therapy is the administration of chelating agents to remove heavy metals from the body. Presumably used here as a treatment for Oleg's Autism symptoms. There is considerable disagreement about this treatment within the medical and the general Autism treatment community, to say the least.

experience coming to this school. The primary thing is that Oleg became more social. Even several months ago, he wouldn't see other people, child or adult, even in close environments, he would see through the person. Now, if someone enters the room, he looks at the person. He tries to look out of the corner of his eyes at what the person is doing. So, he is more interested in other people. He developed new play skills. He will initiate new games, such as chasing. He loves Superman! He does it at home so I see it. He will play with the farm stuff at home. The main thing is that he initiates it. He doesn't know how to finish it, but he initiates it. He became interested in books, he loves to read books. He can't read in English, but he loves to read the books and then explain to me what the main point is. He took the Tarzan book, and explained to me that Tarzan is suffering because he doesn't have any clothes, and it's cold outside! I guess it's not the main point of the book, but he is noticing details and telling me about them.

"His speech has improved in English. He did not lose his Russian, but at the same time his speech improved in English. He understands movies, cartoons mostly. He understands what people say." Mom gives a series of commands and one-step directions that she believed Oleg could follow. Then she goes farther. "Before, maybe half-a-year ago he would not follow even one-step instructions, now he can follow two-step instructions without reminding him to do so. Even more, he can follow instructions in English. If I tell him to bring the book, and take this cup to the kitchen, he'll do it, exactly in the order that I tell him, in English. And that's a big achievement for him.

"He is on a gluten-free, casein-free diet. He is also on a low-carb diet. We went to the gastroenterologist, and it showed that Oleg has inflammation of his digestive tract."

At the beginning of the school year when Oleg was admitted, our second year, we created a Floortime classroom that was more homogeneous in terms of Functional Emotional Developmental Level. The kids in Oleg's age range in this classroom were functioning at Milestones I and II, but spent much of the day struggling to stay regulated. The teacher and the teaching assistants worked unrelentingly to make the classroom work, but it was clear before too long that the teacher and TAs would work themselves to death trying to make this classroom be a productive place for the students before they could actually make that happen. We, the administration, had made a class that no one could possibly make succeed, and we needed to find a solution. Sitting down, we decided to split the class to lower the energy.

We were lucky to have a Teaching Assistant who was up to the challenge of the class.

Alla took on the role of head teacher in a class of children who were for the most part having real difficulty staying regulated. She took a crew of new Teaching Assistants and waded into the problem of making this class work. Miraculously, the kids in the class made real progress, and she helped the Teaching Assistants become among the best Floortime practitioners in the school. It was into this classroom that we brought Oleg. Alla describes him at the time that we presented him to Dr. Greenspan in a case conference.

"Oleg is affectionate and is quite comfortable initiating interactions with adults and sometimes tries to interact with other students. When Oleg approaches staff members, it's usually to ask for a snack or express some desire, or to engage us in pretend play. However, when Oleg expresses his ideas, they are usually unconnected to one another or too vague for us to understand. For example, he may say, 'Is this one there?' without gesturing or explaining what he is referring to. If asked for clarification, Oleg doesn't clarify and instead may repeat the question over and over, and then ask us to repeat it. He used to get really upset if the question or phrase wasn't repeated verbatim.

"It's always so much fun playing with Oleg; he is really creative and adorable. When he does become overexcited, to calm down he usually crawls into someone's arms and wants to snuggle. Oleg has a wonderful sense of humor; right before he screams, he usually looks over at a teacher with a twinkle in his eyes and says in his mom's voice, 'What's all the screaming about?' Or once when I asked him what he was up to because he had that little twinkle in the eyes, he looked and me, smiled and said, 'I'm being sneaky.' "

Alla describes Oleg's functioning at the different Functional Emotional Developmental Milestones at the time of the conference with Dr. Greenspan:

Milestone I: Oleg is usually regulated throughout the day. He does not withdraw into his own world when left alone; in fact, he usually picks up toys and plays with them. However, when Oleg becomes dysregulated, he screams and kicks his legs on the floor. When Oleg wants us to repeat something or wants to communicate an idea that isn't clear enough for us to understand, he becomes extremely upset.

Milestone II: Oleg is easily engaged in a game or a conversation and loves being playful and loves being around others. Sometimes when we call his name, he does not answer, or if we are in the middle of an interaction, he may walk away when it becomes too challenging for him.

Milestone III: Oleg is always intentional in his communication with us. I speak to him in Russian and understand most of the things he says. However, by now a lot of his other teachers and therapists have learned some Russian words, and Oleg is picking up a lot of English words, and he finds ways to express himself in play without relying on words. Oleg's biggest challenge at this level is his lack of using gestures and jumping from subject to subject, or verbalizing a thought that is not connected to anything, as far as we as listeners can understand.

Milestone IV: This is the area where Oleg has the most trouble. Even in an environment where Oleg is most comfortable (a quiet, well-lit room with a lot of small toys, books, clay, or anything that he can manipulate) or during sensory play, he can only open ten to fifteen circles of communication before he abandons the topic, walks away, or loses interest in the conversation or play when asked "W" questions. He can answer a "W" question about something that's in front of him, but not about things that he has to visualize. For example, when Oleg comes up to me and asks, "Is that one there?" in order for me to give him a response I have to ask him, "Where?" or "Who?" He will not answer, and if I give him two options, he'll make a choice but not show much intentionality or interest. But he can answer, "Where should I tickle you?" or "How should we spin?" especially when given options.

The same goes for Oleg's motor planning. He abandons the task of finding pretzels, which he wants, when the cabinet they are in is closed. When asked where the pretzels are, or whether we need a key or a finger to open the door, or "Who should open the door?" or "How can we reach the top shelf where they are kept?" Oleg will not answer and walk away from the challenge. Although, if left to his own devices, I have no doubt that he would solve this problem very quickly.

Milestone V: Oleg is very comfortable with pretend play and often initiates it. The themes he explores most often are animals biting and fighting each other, although he asks or tells me which animals are good and which are bad. Oleg can play doctor, chef, and gold-mining pirate, abilities that were discovered respectively as he bit my finger, put on a chef's hat during counseling, and poked holes in clay during art therapy. The trouble here is that Oleg does not show empathy. While he knows when someone is crying, and why they are upset, he does not know how to react and may still be smiling. When some of his classmates are upset or looking particularly cute, Oleg wants to hug them, but it looks like he is choking them sometimes, and he does not back off when they kick him.

Milestone VI: Oleg is just starting to answer simple "Why" questions if given two options: for example: "Why do you want pretzels, because you are hungry or because you are tired?" Oleg does connect his thoughts and he has said before, "You are crying because I bit you, right?" But, if I asked him, "Why am I upset?" he wouldn't answer. Oleg understands cause and effect; sometimes he does certain things because he knows he'll get a reaction. He mimics other kids' behaviors that he knows get our attention (usually negative). Overall, Oleg understands a lot more than he is able to express to us at this point. He gives us bits and pieces of his thoughts, and we really want to help him connect and verbalize his thoughts.

Today, at the beginning of the new school year, Alla, whose new role at the school is as a member of the newly created Floortime Team, goes to see Oleg for a Floortime session once a day. During the second week of September of Oleg's second year, Alla came to his classroom and sat by him as he worked on a tabletop project. For about a minute he did not notice her sitting right beside him, but once he did, he turned to her, reached for her hand, put it gently on the side of his face, and returned to the project. She asked if he wanted help, and when he said that he did, she helped him with the project, asking him if he wanted to draw the eyes, or paste googly-eyes on, if he wanted glue or tape, all in Russian, so he could work alongside his new friends. Then, it came to a place where he had to write his name on the work, and Alla tried to help him as he struggled to take the marker in his hand and write. But he couldn't even begin. He almost could not make the marker touch the page, as his motor-planning problems, as well as anxiety about not keeping up with his peers, interfered. Alla tried to support him, and dotted out his name, but even this was too much at that moment. He got upset, and threw the marker. He made increasingly loud vocalizations. He got up and paced. He began to yell at Alla, inches from her face, "Go away!"

"You want me to go away?" she asked.

"No." Oleg replied. He got louder and louder, and Alla helped him into a quieter space where he could work it out. He began to say, "It happened, it happened."

"You're right, it happened. You did get upset, and you did yell, and you did not like it, then we came out here, and now we're talking in this quiet room."

"Loud. Mark. Marker!"

"Loud," Alla said.

"Say it didn't happen! Say it didn't happen!"

"It did happen. You screamed. It was loud."

"Loud. Screamed." Oleg was really upset.

"You were sad." Alla said it in Russian and English, because while it was helpful in the moment for her to know what was wrong, in the long run he would be mostly with English speakers, and would need to be able to speak to them about his feelings.

This went on for several minutes: Oleg fragmented by the disconnect between his feelings and his inability to hold the images and the sequence of the world in his head, and Alla trying to help him to connect things. Finally, he was able to pull himself together, and said, "I got loud, I screamed in Mark's room. Sad."

He got up, and joined his friends in the class, as they went through the obstacle course the teachers had set up.

## Sensory and Motor Strengths and Challenges as Understood and Described by the Rebecca School Staff

### Visual Spatial:

- Appears to have difficulty shifting his focus from one object to another, an essential skill in the classroom. For instance, he may be able to focus on a person when far away from them on a swing, but loses them as they approach him. This difficulty shifting his attention quickly may account for some of his dysregulation in a high-energy classroom with several other highly kinetic boys.

### Auditory:

- This is an area of relative strength. Oleg will seek out spoken language rather than gestural communication, even when he is having difficulty with translation. He does not appear to avoid loud environments, in fact, he will add significantly to the auditory confusion when he is dysregulated.

### Proprioceptive:

- Oleg seeks proprioceptive input, jumping and bouncing on equipment and hiding in confined spaces like a barrel in the sensory gym. He seeks deep pressure in hugs from people whom he loves and trusts.

### Vestibular:

- Oleg seeks sensory input, but gets rapidly dysregulated with vestibular input. He will swing linearly, but dislikes spinning. He will run around, and as he becomes increasingly dysregulated, he becomes more frantic. At times like these he is difficult to calm down. This mixed pattern, of sensory seeking leading to sensory overstimulation, makes it difficult to work with Oleg around sensory issues.

## Tactile:

- No tactile sensitivities observed.

## Oral:

- Oleg seeks oral input, particularly when dysregulated.

## Motor Processing and Planning:

- Oleg is physically fit and able to move through his environment fluidly, but has difficulty with ideational motor planning. For example, he will have difficulty moving something capable of holding his weight across a room to reach an object he wants that is above his reach. He will, instead, try to stand on any object already near his desired object, even if it would not support him. He will also perform feats that are potentially dangerous to him. He will stand on the top railing of climbing equipment where a fall would cause him real harm. (*Note:* Since the time of the conference, Oleg's safety awareness has become much greater.)

## Rebecca School Program in Place Before Consulting with Dr. Greenspan

*Floortime: 3–4 x 20 min./day, Individual, in the classroom, with teacher or one specific teaching assistant, primarily.*

*Speech: 3 x 30 min./week, Individual.*

- Goals include improving Oleg's tolerance to oral-sensory input and expanding circles of communication. Focus of therapy is facilitating acquisition of a functional English vocabulary.

**OT: 3 x 30 min./week, Individual.**

- A sensory diet has been implemented in the classroom that includes brushing, deep touch massage, hugging, wheelbarrow walking, jumping on trampoline, and classical music.

**PT: 2 x 30 min./week, Individual.**

- Improve attention and motor-planning and sequencing capabilities to allow for increased problem solving in the physical domain.
- Work with a large therapy ball while regulating the space between the therapist and himself using gestures and facial expressions.
- Work on a four- to five-step obstacle course, while maintaining attention to task, with minimal assistance from therapist.

**Music Therapy: 1 x 30 min./week.**

**Art Therapy: 2 x 20 min./week, with two peers.**

## Dr. Greenspan's Recommendations

Oleg who is seven-and-a-half years old, comes from Russia, and has a history of a diagnosis of ASD. He can be focused and regulated, but gets easily overloaded and dysregulated and he can bite and get aggressive. Sometimes his tantrums can last a long time. He also can remain regulated for long periods of time. He is very sweet and can engage, which is a real strength of his. He is not yet persistent in his engagement and doesn't yet have a real understanding of other people's needs or emotions, so he can over-hug another child, for example. Oleg can be purposeful and interact with words and gestures, but doesn't yet have a continuous flow.

Oleg can sequence and problem solve, but does not yet have the continuous flow. At school, he can get fifteen circles; at home, he may get many more if it's something he's really interested in—ten to fifteen minutes or more. However, he doesn't have the range and flexibility to apply this in a variety of contexts or activities and settings. We want to really work on that continuous flow.

Oleg can use ideas creatively, but here, too, he doesn't have a wide range yet. He can pretend a little bit, but doesn't show a lot of emotional range, like pretending about anger, sadness, surprise, etc. There are not yet rich, creative dramas. He can connect ideas together, but is inconsistent. Since he speaks Russian fluently, but not yet English, it's a little hard for him to be consistent with all the staff. At home, he does answer "Why" questions some of the time and in Russian he can do it with multiple-choice help some of the time, but is not yet consistent at the "Why" level or even with some of the other "W" questions. We want to work on making his language a real two-way communication so he can process it more effectively.

## Constitutional and Maturational Variations

Processing difficulties contribute to Oleg's challenges. He has language and auditory-processing challenges, more difficult on the receptive side than on the expressive side. He has clear motor-planning and sequencing challenges, as nicely described by the Rebecca School staff. He is very sensory overreactive and can crave sensory input a little bit. However, he's mostly overreactive and gets overloaded easily.

Visual-spatial processing difficulties are a big part of Oleg's challenges, and he tends to get lost in the trees and overfocus at times. He doesn't see the big picture. He also has a lot of difficulty with body awareness and a sense of his body in space. He could use a lot of work on the visual-spatial side.

## Prognosis

Oleg's prognosis is best indicated by his learning curve over the next few months and years with an appropriate intervention program. As that curve continues on an upward trend, his prognosis for continued improvement remains very good. Oleg shows lots of strengths because of what he can do some of the time, even if he doesn't do it all of the time, like his conversations with Mom about Tarzan. This was a beautiful illustration of what Oleg can do. He has lots of potential and the fact that he is mastering a second language (English) a bit and likes books and has things he likes to talk about is a good sign. We want to see if we can get that learning curve sloping upward more and more and get it going at a faster rate.

## Game Plan

The program that the staff has for Oleg is excellent and everyone is sensitive to his needs. The fact that he loves school is a wonderful sign. Mother really enjoys talking with Oleg, which is wonderful. I would like to suggest a few other things to make this program even better. Because emotional regulation and language are big issues for Oleg and because I think he is capable of moving more quickly, I'd like there to be a primary person or two who are Oleg's main people who speak both Russian and English. If possible, have a volunteer come in (someone that Mom might recruit) or a graduate or undergraduate student from Russia who could spend a lot of time with Oleg, along with the staff. The goal for that person would be to train them up to be a great Floortimer. It would be hard to do the Floortime with Oleg as well as he is capable of unless the person can speak Russian with him. Oleg's teacher should do three twenty-minute Floortime sessions with Oleg and the student or volunteer could come in to do another three or four twenty-minute Floortime sessions. This will really get his thinking cooking and get him solid at the "Why" and other "W" question levels and to expand his ability to talk about his feelings. He will get a lot more interaction with people to learn the non-verbal signaling system so he doesn't over-squeeze people and know that he is hurting someone, etc. This comes from lots of interaction and where the child doesn't have this nonverbal signaling system, it has to be from one-on-one interactions with a very animated person using lots of gesturing who is also engaging Oleg in verbal discussions. The time could start off with a book or character from a book that he is interested in and build the interaction from that, like when Tarzan is happy or sad or angry or surprised, etc. Get some Tarzan characters or other characters he likes and use them as a basis of beginning pretending. Or you can work on making up stories about the characters he likes. Engage him in long one-on-one conversations during these Floortime sessions (about seven per day) and in six months I think we could see huge progress in Oleg.

The other staff who are working with Oleg should help him to master talking in English. Don't let his speaking Russian make you cautious about your expectations for what Oleg can do in English. At his age, he can still master English interactively. Let him experience some of the immersion language work, but around things he is passionate about, something he really wants. He will master English more quickly that way. I want him to retain thinking and speaking in Russian, but I also want him to learn English as a second language and do it more quickly than he is currently doing so he can make full use of all the people who want to talk to him.

Oleg is a good candidate to do the *Thinking Goes to School* program, initially in Russian until he becomes more fluent in English. I recommend adding this to his daily routine, doing at least two twenty-minute sessions a day. I think he would benefit enormously from these exercises.

Having Oleg spend time with the older, Russian-English speaking child at the school is a wonderful idea and I recommend starting this right away. There should be a facilitator present, preferably someone who speaks Russian. This could be done for three or four sessions a day, or at least a couple of sessions. They can become buddies and converse in Russian and play together. It would be interesting to videotape those sessions periodically because it would be a unique opportunity to help him learn both Russian and English and interact with another child. It would also be useful for the older child because he would be mentoring a younger child. This is a terrific idea, and I would do it right away.

At home, I'd like mother to do at least two or three twenty-minute Floortime sessions in the evening, in addition to teaching him to read and doing other more structured activities. Oleg's father should do at least two twenty-minute sessions where he plays with him in the evening. It's important for a boy, particularly one who tends to be aggressive, to be close to his father. He has to be close to both his mother and his father. Dad should come in to get some coaching from the staff on doing Floortime so he is comfortable with doing this with Oleg.

The screen time for Oleg (i.e., TV, computer) needs to be cut down to no more than a half hour a day.

The keys for Oleg are more Floortime, long, long conversations with more emotional range and flexibility, bringing in help if needed, more time with Daddy at home, Mom working on Russian and English, working with Oleg on feelings (not just once a week in the psychology sessions) at home, and for him to really feel that he has a primary connection with one or two people at school, including the older Russian-speaking student. We want to see lots of progress over the next six months. I think we can bring Oleg to a much higher level.

## Chapter 10

# Your Son: Priceless

"On Friday evening, I took him out for a bite to eat, and I had my credit card on the table. He picked it up and looked at me and said,

'Restaurant bill on your MasterCard: twenty dollars,

Ice cream after: five dollars,

Dinner out with your son: Priceless.' "

Mom begins her discussion of her delightful son with her absolute joy at her son's wit, humor, and powers of mimicry. This charm, which so endears her ten-year-old son, Dan, to her, makes him a favorite with everyone. But, Mom also tells about what her darkest moments are with Dan. "We were on vacation a couple of weeks ago and he was at his very worst. He was among many typical kids of all ages, so he was doing things that were really fun for kids. But it became very, very overwhelming to him, and he wound up pushing a child, a sixteen-year-old boy, into the lake at night, and the kid could have been killed, he hit his head, and got a big bruise on it. He proceeded to exhibit all the regressive behaviors I have seen over the years, he would urinate in public, he cursed a lot. Continuing with the idea of the best and worst of him, on the night he pushed the kid in the lake, he was completely in a downward spiral, he looked at me and said, 'Mom, I wish I could be a normal kid.'" Mom continued to speak of her lowest moments with Dan. "A couple of years ago we were adjusting his medications and he told me that he wanted to kill me, and told me how he would do it in graphic detail. And, we had to hospitalize him for about a week. So, that was Daniel at his worst."

Mom spoke about her pregnancy with Dan and his early days. "My pregnancy was complicated by severe preeclampsia in week twenty-six. He was born in week twenty-seven. He was born weighing one pound, twelve ounces and had the worst complication of prematurity that they have, which is a grade four inter-ventricular hemorrhage. This resulted in hydrocephalous, nine spinal taps, ninety-one days in the NICU (neonatal intensive care unit), and all the other preemie annoyances, but obviously the most severe being the brain injury. I was very ill. I was sick for two weeks in intensive care. I had visual loss for nine weeks. I took him home three months after he was born on an oxygen tank and a heart monitor. Basically, the first three years of his life were filled with various therapists. He started early intervention at birth, with physical therapy, then we introduced occupational therapy and speech. At the age of three-and-a-half he started a full-time day program. Daniel, in addition to all of his behavioral issues has cerebral palsy, a left hemiparesis, and it has really manifested itself primarily in the lack of use of his left hand. So, all of the developmental milestones were seriously delayed, if we saw them at all."

When I first met Dan, he was the epitome of a carefully dressed and coiffed Upper East Side Manhattan kid. He had on a button-down shirt, a red V-neck sweater, and khakis. When Mom left the treatment room, Dan and I got down on the floor to duke it out, as we explored his favorite topic, the WWE professional wrestling. Grrrrrr!

I grabbed the Flash, and he grabbed Han Solo, and we played out a steel cage match he had just watched on pay-per-view. He narrated. "*Ooo, he has the Undertaker in a Suplex! And, he slams him down!*" My character, the Undertaker, looked like he suffered at least a neck and back injury. "*Now he bounces off the rail, and here comes the Clothesline!*" The Clothesline dropped the Flash/Undertaker to the canvas. "*He goes for the pin!*" His character jumped on mine to end the match. "But, the Undertaker kicks out at the last moment," I said. And with that, my character kicked his character off and bounced up, saved from defeat. Dan was surprised, but able to come back, beating the Undertaker again and again, only to have him kick out of the pin again and again. Finally, the match ended when he began to show signs of his frustration, and the Undertaker was beaten into submission.

My general impression was of a kid capable of staying regulated for at least some of the time, under the right circumstances, with some resilience to adversity, but with limits to his flexibility. He was engaged and related, but under the right circumstances which gave him considerable control. He seemed to be able to communicate around themes of aggression and anger, but I had difficulty steering him into other emotional streams. He was able to problem solve, and sometimes join his ideas with mine, but again, he could not do this across all themes. He was able to play in a representative way, but only had pockets of strength in symbolic play. He could be logical, and connect ideas, but again, this ability was dependent upon the circumstance. I had only spent a little time with Dan, and hadn't had time to get to know him in all his richness, but I knew that we had an appropriate classroom where he would have peers, and so we offered him and his family acceptance to Rebecca School, and he began when we first opened our doors in September of 2006.

The classroom teacher describes the warm and funny child she sees. "We named the classroom 'The Jokers' because Dan has a joke every two minutes. Any situation that occurs in the classroom, off the top of his head he comes out with a joke. And, today he actually told us, 'I have a lot of jokes in my head, but the right situation has to happen in order for them to come out.' He came in September, very happy. I visited the house before the school year started, and he greeted me with a whistle, I guess saying that I was attractive to him. I said, 'Thanks for the warm welcome.' He is very social in terms of people who come by the classroom. He likes to greet them. He says, 'Hi, how are you? My name is Daniel.' It's appropriate at times, but then if he notices something about them, maybe their weight or maybe something on their face, he'll make an inappropriate comment. One was, someone was coming around on a tour and he said, 'Hear about that new acne medicine?' I think he was trying to be funny, but he doesn't know that that was an inappropriate way to do it, so we're working on appropriate ways to say things."

"He's very active, he likes to make friends, and he loves movement situations. He likes to always be moving. The problem is, if he moves too much he gets overstimulated. He has this thing with wrestling, wrestlers are his life, so if he gets overstimulated he begins to do those moves. If we don't comply with what he's asking, he becomes dysregulated, and we begin to see certain behaviors start to come out. We try to move the wrestling into other things, but if he can't do the wrestling at that time, it's hard to get through to him. That's when we'll experience some of the behaviors Mom spoke about, with the urinating in inappropriate places, and swearing."

The occupational therapist describes Dan as having, "difficulty modulating input. He has very good visual-spatial skills in terms of being able to copy, write, and draw. When he searches for objects he isn't hindered at all. He has problems with social body awareness. He is clumsy. He has low tone. His bilateral skills are not what they should be. We are constantly prompting him to use his nondominant hand. He will attempt fine-motor tasks, but if he can't get it right the first time he will either abandon the task, or lately, he has begun to ask for help. He is not smooth and coordinated by any means, but he knows it, and he tries very hard." The physical therapist adds, "He demonstrates decreased endurance, muscularly, with short bursts of immense strength, but he is unable to maintain that. He has decreased balance standing and sitting, secondary to some decreased strength around his core." The occupational therapist continues, "His vestibular processing, I don't want to say it's poor, because balance postural reactions come into play. He will get on a swing, he'll move in all planes, but he will fall off." Mom jumps in, "And he doesn't cry. I mention it because he has always been like this, and it seems different from other kids. He can get hurt, and bounce up laughing. He doesn't seem to feel the pain."

"He is overreactive to sound, particularly the fire alarm," says the occupational therapist. The classroom teacher adds, "If a child in the classroom makes a loud noise, Dan will get up and make a gesture like he is going to hit the child, but then he doesn't, and he'll use his words instead of becoming physical."

"Obviously, Dan is a very social and expressive child," says his speech therapist, "but we do work on pragmatics. Having him work on appropriate peer interactions, resolving conflicts appropriately with other peers or staff members, exhibiting self-control, and he is able to identify, basically, all the correct behaviors. He knows what he's supposed to say and what he's supposed to do. Outside of the situation we pretend together. We do a mock interaction, and he is able to do it appropriately within the context, but outside in a stressful situation he has trouble remembering what he is supposed to do. I have him in a dyad with another child at a similar cognitive level, and they are able to do things together, make things together, and take turns. The other day, Dan was able to reflect with the other child on something they had done together, and plan for the future something they would do. He just really enjoys socializing with other children. He just needs a prompt to know how to approach other kids sometimes."

### Sensory and Motor Strengths and Challenges as Understood and Described by the Rebecca School Staff

*Visual Spatial:*

- Demonstrates decreased whole body awareness with relation to his extremities and trunk in space.
- Will at times attune to his body and move around people and objects, often appears to be unaware of his path of movement and any obstacles.

*Auditory:*

- Easily overstimulated.
- Finds loud noise very distracting. The fire alarm at school is intolerable, for instance, and he will sometimes threaten another student if he or she is being too loud.

*Proprioceptive:*

- Responds well to deep pressure, as this helps him place his body in space.

### Vestibular:

- Responds well to vestibular input.
- Demonstrates good static sitting balance and fair, dynamic sitting balance (when sitting on a moving surface Dan has difficulty maintaining his balance without assistance).
- Demonstrates good static standing balance. Dan requires close supervision during dynamic standing balance activities (walking over uneven surfaces) to prevent loss of balance and falls.

### Tactile:

- No tactile defensiveness noted.

### Feeding:

- No unusual food preferences noted.

### Motor Processing and Planning:

- Often requires verbal cuing to smoothly and efficiently execute gross-motor tasks including reaching for a ball or moving a piece of equipment in the gym to create an obstacle course.
- Instead of moving around obstacles Dan will choose to flop down on the pillow or mat, demonstrating his decreased ability to motor plan a path around the obstacle.

### Rebecca School Program in Place Before Consulting with Dr. Greenspan

*Floortime: 4-6 x 20 min./day, in a dyad or a group, in the classroom, with teacher and teaching assistants, primarily.*

- Dan is capable of sophisticated thinking and expression, up to Levels VII and VIII, but staff works often at Level V with him, in fantasy play.

**Speech: 2 x 30 min./week, 1 x Individual, 1 x group of 3.**

- Therapy mainly focuses on developing social skills with peers and staff members, problem solving in various everyday situations, and critical thinking skills. Other areas addressed intermittently are articulation and oral-motor skills to improve his lateral emission of airflow for sounds.

**OT: 3 x 30 min./week, Individual, 1 x 30 min./week, group of 3 (movement group with OT and PT), 1 x 30 min./week, group of 5 (movement group with OT and PT).**

- Therapy has focused on helping Dan improve his poor bilateral coordination, poor grading of movement, decreased postural and balance reactions and difficulty modulating his responses to unexpected or over excitatory situations.

**PT: 3 x 30 min./week, Individual, 1 x 30 min./week, group of 3 (movement group with OT and PT), 1 x 30 min./week, group of 5 (movement group with OT and PT).**

- Reciprocal stepping pattern, without handrail, for stairs, fluidity, increased stability.

**Music Therapy: 1 x 30 min./week.**

**Art Therapy: 2 x 20 min./week, with two peers.**

### Dr. Greenspan's Recommendations

Dan, a young boy who is almost eleven years old, has a history of having had some perinatal challenges that left him with a brain hemorrhage and left hemiparesis. He had some initial challenges with language, but then took off. He currently has impulse control and behavioral challenges, but he also has a lot of strengths. Dan can take an interest in things, but it's hard for him to regulate himself when he gets overloaded and frustrated. He employs impulsive behavior in these situations, but then can feel bad about it and wishes he hadn't. He is engaged and likable. He doesn't have the full range of emotions; for instance, he has trouble handling loss, and his ability to handle competition is constricted. He can be purposeful and get into two-way, purposeful interactions, but he is limited in his emotional range.

He can sequence and problem solve, but in a limited emotional range. Motor planning is a challenge for him. He hasn't quite come to grips with his body and what he can and cannot do. Dan can use ideas creatively, meaningfully, and off of affect. He has a tendency to put his feelings into action, which bypasses the idea level, but he is improving in this area. We can help him expand his emotional range through imaginative play or making up stories, as is age appropriate. Indirectly, through drawings, for example, we can help him deal with the emotions of loss, sadness, competition, aggression, and other emotions he finds difficult. He can connect ideas and answer "Why" questions, but cannot elaborate on them. He gets caught in obsessive and nonlogical thinking. Although he is improving in this area, it's not as well established as we would like to see in emotional situations and when the feelings are strong.

Overall, it's hard for Dan to do higher level thinking, i.e., multicausal and gray-area thinking. If we can get him into the gray-area and subtle thinking, he will overcome the all-or-nothing type of thinking which fuels the obsessive thinking tendencies. He shows flashes of insight and reflective thinking and we have to be careful about being charmed by those flashes of insight because we have to help him do this across the full range of emotions. His lack of ability to do this is what contributes to the problems he has with magical and all-or-nothing thinking.

### Constitutional and Maturational Variations

Dan has language challenges in the area of thinking. While it is clear that he has some strengths in language, he is not as strong at applying this language in his thought about a subject as we would expect him to be for his age. He clearly has motor-planning and sequencing challenges, most likely related to his physical challenges. He is sensory overreactive and can get overloaded, particularly in loud environments. Like some of the children we have already discussed in this book, he is also sensory craving in some modalities. So he is sensitive to sound, and tries to shut it out, but he seeks proprioceptive and vestibular feedback at times. Dan has challenges in visual-spatial processing, and we need to help strengthen this area for him.

### Game Plan

Overall, as a general principle, Dan needs to develop the ability for higher levels of thinking across the full range of emotions and situations. We attribute more to him than he is actually capable of, and allow ourselves to be charmed by him. Thus, we end up not helping him enough to do these higher levels of thinking across the full range of situations. He should have at least four half-hour Floortime sessions a day with a skilled mental health person or a person who is skilled in helping him play out and dramatize and explore the whole drama of his life and his feelings. At home, focus on what he's feeling about things. Play the Thinking About Tomorrow game where Dan visualizes what's going to happen tomorrow, both good and bad things, and pictures what he will like and not like. He should anticipate how he and others will feel in those good and bad situations, how he typically reacts when he's in those situations; and alternative ways of acting. For example, he can talk about situations in school where he gets aggressive or impulsive and describe what happens when he gets frustrated. He can describe the situation or even draw it or act it out like a pretend drama. He should come up with the ideas himself, but you can ask the questions to help him think of alternatives, such as, "Well, what do you think you could do differently the next time, instead of ___?" Playing this game every day will help Dan become a "poet of his feelings" and prepare him for situations ahead of time. We don't want to get to the alternatives too quickly because we want to focus on the feelings. Do a lot of anticipatory thinking as well as exploratory thinking.

Dan is a good candidate for a good mental health program. There should be male influences in his life at school as well as at home, for example a Big Brother-type program. It's also important that Dan have a very strong program in body awareness and control and a strong program in visual-spatial thinking. He should have OT for at least two twenty-minute sessions each day working on body awareness and control and coordination, with a lot of cerebellar, balance, and sequencing activities. He is a good candidate for a lot of rhythmicity and timing work. He needs to strengthen his visual-spatial processing and is a good candidate for *Thinking Goes to School* exercises. He should have at least two twenty-minute sessions each day working on the visual-spatial exercises from the book.

Regarding academics for Dan: Everything should be thinking based.

If there is one overarching principle, it is to try to not work so much on helping him in a rote way to learn what is and isn't appropriate behavior. He needs to work on the more fundamental issues of putting his impulses and feelings into ideas and then to sequence and problem solve, and understanding the why and how of things. Have much more open-ended dialogues, not just what do you do or don't do in this situation or that situation. Otherwise, he will remain in the state he's in now—a child with flashes of insight and brilliance, but with impulse control issues.

### Rebecca School's Response to Dr. Greenspan's Recommendations

Over a year has passed since this conference call. In order to make Daniel's program at Rebecca School better, we have combined two of the older classrooms, giving Dan a wider range of peers with whom to interact. The noise level in the classroom certainly did not decrease, but as Dan has become more flexible and better at self-regulation, he does not mind it. There are even two girls in his class now, which Dan handles more maturely than any of his peers. As he grows and becomes more acutely aware of his own complex emotions and thoughts and has to deal with occurances that are unpredictable to him, he struggles. Despite our efforts to supply Dan and his classmates with male TAs to provide that "big brother" role, we have not been successful. While the other boys enjoy their boisterous and rough "brothers" in the classroom, Dan continues to struggle with jumping into the mix with them. He'll watch them and laugh, but prefers more cerebral pastimes. This charming young man truly touches everyone who works him, as he becomes a "poet of his feelings." He learns through relationships about what makes people happy, sad, angry, dissappointed, jealous, uncomfortable, or embarrassed, and so on, by experiencing those emotions and by being made aware of when his peers, therapists, and teachers react with those same feelings. Dan is on the way, but we need to continue to expand our support and our program so the he can continue to capitalize on his wit, his joyful enthusiasm, and his gift to make people like him.

# Chapter 11

# Dancing with the Stars

"William has an older brother, named Jonah, and he came right after Jonah was born. It was a challenging pregnancy. My wife was on bed rest for the last four months. There were no issues in terms of how he was born, without any drugs or anesthesia, no drugs, except to help induce labor. He was average weight, his APGAR scores were fine. He came home with us, our first one was a preemie, so that was a big deal. When he came home with us, there was nothing unusual, for about the first four or five months at least, nothing that I noticed. Around the sixth month, he began to do some things that were very interesting. Around his sixth month, for instance, his connections; he only got connected with my wife. But, when he would look at her, it was like he would look into her, not at her, not with her, that would be the best way to say it." Mom adds, "He just had a very intense stare, but he wouldn't look at anyone else."

Dad continued, "Another thing, he had a shrill scream. It wasn't like the other kids. It was very high-pitched, and it wasn't necessarily that something was wrong, it was like this release of tension, is the best way I can phrase it. We also noticed that he wasn't doing what his brother was doing at the different months. Like he would be doing less at nine months than his brother had done at nine months, and his brother was premature, so William should have been doing more. We began to notice that." Mom says, "He never actually got to the talking phase. He babbled, and then that went away, around eight, nine, ten months, that went away. And at that point, we just didn't know what his voice was like. He never really developed into talking. Around that time, eleven months, we really started noticing there was something wrong. He would just stare at the TV, be completely engrossed in the TV, be completely engrossed in something on the computer screen, and he started spinning at that time. He would spin objects."

Dad picked up, "He never played with a toy appropriately. Every toy that he had, he would spin. It didn't make a difference what the toy was. If the toy had wheels, great, because he would spin the wheels on the toy. If the toy didn't have wheels, let's say it was a square toy, he was very ingenious, because he would find some way to make everything spin, even things that were not round. In order for him to play with it, ultimately, everything had to spin. The better it spun, the more he liked it. For his first birthday, my wife got him a top, and he would just look at that top spin for inordinate amounts of time. Also during this time, he would bang his head. At that time we had an iron radiator, and one day he banged his head on that, and after that he didn't bang his head anymore." Mom corrects Dad a little by saying, "After that, he banged his head on the pillow. So we knew he wasn't not sensible." Mom and Dad laughed together.

"He learned to walk really well around fifteen months. He did all of that really well. But the first thing he began to do was spin. Once he could spin himself around in a circle, he would just spin. It was at that point that I said that he was spinning, and I knew where I had seen spinning before, because my mother used to work with autistic children," said Dad, referring to William's grandmother. "So when I saw the spinning I said, 'Oh my god, he's on that spectrum. He most likely has Autism.' Mom and I had a conversation at that point, and we looked to get him evaluated. Personality-wise, he has a very strong will. You would tell him something, and he would ignore it. When he goes after something, he goes after it, but what made it unique was that you could not connect with him to tell him not to do something. The thing that was dangerous was that we would go for walks with him in the neighborhood, and the tendency was for him to bolt off. The other children wouldn't run away, but you had to watch him because he would run away."

Mom says, "Around the ten-month time we knew something was wrong because he began acting like he couldn't hear. You would call his name, and one time I went into his room, and there was no one else in the room and I got next to the crib and I banged on the floor, and he didn't budge. We understood there was something wrong and we went to get help."

"We went to early intervention, and my mother kind of told us some things to do. We didn't really listen to my mother, and we should have, but we did ultimately listen to her," Dad says laughing softly. "My mother kind of plays in because she runs a really large daycare, and she had seen a lot of stuff, but she wanted us to come to terms with it before she got involved. She began to suggest things to us, but she wasn't sure how we would deal with it. She wanted to give us time.

"We got early intervention services involved, and it was the most horrific thing I have ever seen. We took a child who I could see, without any training, was on the spectrum, and we took him to their best psychologist, who has a center and she said, 'You know what, he'll probably grow out of it. It's too early to tell if anything's wrong, give him some time, maybe about a year, and he'll probably snap out of it. Lots of children go through this particular phase. I don't see anything that's noticeably different.' We made appointments with two different neurologists, and they told us, 'There's no doubt, he is on the spectrum. You need to make as much noise as possible, because they are not going to give you anything if you don't.' They alerted us and told us we really had to get on the ball."

"He's been getting ABA services since he was two. He has progressed a lot. Before he got any services, he was totally internalized. No interaction, no attachment with his brother, the only person he attached to was my wife, really. And everything else was nonexistent. He began to interact with his surroundings. Then he started talking." Then Dad began to talk about a strange pattern they noticed. "William was getting intensive ABA, six hours a day at home. And it was really intense, but it seemed like it was going in but nothing was happening. But then, he would get sick, and not get ABA for a while, and he would come back, and he would have developed some new skill, or make a milestone. It happened four times. Up until he got to the Rebecca School, he had plateaued. So they would do really intensive things around language, but it wasn't until he came to Rebecca School that we actually heard him speak. He had 200 words, but he never used the words spontaneously. Words are just beginning to pour out. I would definitely attribute that to what has been happening here, because it wasn't happening with the services he was receiving at home."

His mom continued. "His best communication is that he is now using his words, when he is calm and when he is getting what he wants. He'll say, 'I want milk, I want TV.' Recently he did an excellent job. He came upstairs, the TV is downstairs, he came upstairs to me, and he was about to scream, and I put my hand up and stopped him, and I said, 'Use words.' He said, 'Come Moot,' I'm called Moot, Mother, he took me downstairs and pointed to the video and said, 'Elmo.' And then I was about to get a videotape, and he said, 'Firefighter, I want Firefighter.' The tape he wanted was the Elmo Firefighter tape. The worst is that when he is frustrated he will just scream. He will come up to you and just scream. That used to be very typical of him.

The parents describe him as very gentle. "He has a two-year-old sister, and she will just come up to him and jump all over him, and he will just push her off. He will put up with an awful lot of abuse from her," Mom says. Dad adds, "His personality is very mellow, very easygoing, very fun, he never would do anything aggressive toward her," referring to the little sister. "So very gentle. But if you deny him yogurt, it's a whole different story!" Dad says laughing.

William is a tiny, wiry bundle of very strong sinew and movement. He has an anxious look in his eyes, and when I first met him, he carried a blanket everywhere he went. (He just gave up the blanket!) On that first day, when Dad got down to play with him, I could see the stubbornness and the avoidance the parents spoke of. Dad was not able to engage him around any symbolic toys, and he was only successful capturing William's attention when he took a light and sound toy, featuring a pop-up Burt, Ernie, Cookie Monster, and Oscar the Grouch, and let William push the buttons that made them pop up and sing. William got absorbed in the toy, and the room slowly fell silent, except for the sound of Oscar singing, "I love trash! Anything dirty or dingy or dusty."

I thought that I would try to see if I could get William to play, and lay down on the floor near the toys. Despite all of my best effort, my high affect, my trying as hard as I could to see what he was interested in, and then use that, William would not budge. I was loud with large affect, and that pushed him away. I was low and slow, being quiet, and he acted as if I had disappeared. Finally, I moved quietly toward him with a fluffy stuffed monkey, and spoke through the toy about the monkey giving him a kiss. As the monkey moved toward him he turned a cheek to it, and leaned forward, intentionally to make the cheek available. As the monkey kissed his cheek, he smiled, ever so slightly, and I knew, that he was tough, but he was there. He gave us the challenge, and showed us that with the right combination of sensory and fantasy, he would play with us.

Mom has also taken advantage of the parent training offered at Rebecca School. At the beginning of the four-week course, Mom was very timid, she is by nature a quiet, self-effacing person, but by week three she was beginning to come into her own in her Floortime sessions with her son. Other members of the group began to notice her natural abilities, and she was able to offer much material and emotional support to them as they struggled with their children. In the last live-coaching session of the training, Mom and William went back and forth in play in a way that no one could have anticipated on that first day, almost a year ago, when all he would do was listen to Oscar pop up and sing.

### Sensory and Motor Strengths and Challenges as Understood and Described by the Rebecca School Staff

*Visual Spatial:*

- Good visual-spatial awareness.
- Visual-spatial processing is a relative strength.

*Auditory:*

- Easily overstimulated.
- Overreactive to the sounds of the classroom.

- Often has his hands over his ears.
- At home he does not like the hair clippers, the blender, or the vacuum cleaner.

### Proprioceptive:

- Enjoys physical activity with proprioceptive input.
- Loves to bounce.
- Loves to dance.

### Vestibular:

- Enjoys swinging in a linear plane.
- Seeks vestibular.

### Tactile:

- Seeks varied tactile feedback.
- Will curl up in a bin of rice and beans.

### Oral Motor:

- Grinds his teeth.
- Screams. As screaming increases, teeth grinding decreases.
- Overreactive to certain foods.

### Motor Processing and Planning:

- Motor processing and planning are relative strengths.

### Rebecca School Program in Place Before Consulting with Dr. Greenspan

*Floortime: 4–6 x 20 min./day, Individual, in the classroom, with teacher or one specific teaching assistant, primarily.*

*Speech: 3 x 30 min./week, Individual.*

*OT: 2 x 30 min./week, Individual.*

*Music Therapy: 1 x 30 min./week.*

*Art Therapy: 2 x 20 min./week, with two peers.*

## Dr. Greenspan's Recommendations

William, a little boy who is almost six years old, has a history of being diagnosed with ASD. He was in an ABA program where his receptive language improved, but the expressive language did not. He had plateaued until he started with Rebecca School, and he has really started to take off. He can focus and attend. He can get dysregulated and aggressive, but that has lessened in recent months. He can engage with real warmth. However, we want to sustain this for longer periods with more circles.

William can be purposeful and get into back-and-forth interactions with others. He's really ripe to go into the continuous flow where we get ten, fifteen, or twenty circles in a row. Everyone should keep interactions going with him as long as possible, both at school or at home. He can sequence and problem solve, and we want to see more continuous flow here, too.

William is really beginning to use his ideas, with short phrases and back-and-forth interactions. He is beginning to do some pretend play, like dressing up in Daddy's shoes and clothes at home and feeding and bathing a doll at school. We want to really take advantage of this wonderful window of opportunity and build on this. While building on this, we want to make sure that he is in control, that he is the boss during the play.

William is getting ready to connect his ideas together. So now you can begin throwing into his interactions questions like "Should I hold you tight?" Show him the difference so he gets the concept. "Who's going to open the door? You or me?" Get your foot stuck in the door and you can get lots of circles going around going to the door. Hold off on "Why" questions for now, but if the opportunity arises, you can try it, giving him multiple choices (good one first, silly one second).

In summary, we want to build on what you are already doing in the way I just described. He needs more pure one-on-one Floortime with teachers, aides, and he needs more pure one-on-one Floortime at home. Take advantage of this window of opportunity, and get his communication and world of ideas cooking. I expect great things from him, and you will all be very pleased with his progress. Take advantage of his mixed sensory reactivity by letting him talk a lot around the movement he likes, like being Superman, but we need to protect him from the overload. To do this we will have him in settings that are more one-on-one and quiet more of the time than we are doing now. Gradually, we can get him used to the more noisy environments, but we want him at his best most of the time. Focus should be on circles of communication and imagination. He will then learn to be more patient. While you are waiting with him, communicate with him using gestures or facial expressions. No child is good at waiting until you get the continuous flow going; then they become good waiters.

Over the next three to four months, we want to get him to where his best moments are happening ninety-nine percent of the time, then we can go on to the next goal.

## Game Plan

There should be close coordination between the school and home programs, with the parents and staff communicating on a regular basis. At school, in the different therapies (art, drama, classroom, speech, OT, etc.), there should be at least a total of six, one-on-one Floortime sessions for twenty or thirty minutes each in a quiet space where he can bring out his best. Have some pretend play items and do some Floortime where we get involved in pretend play with gestures and words. See how many circles you can get and keep going. Have imaginative materials or create pretend play scenarios in art, the classroom or the sensory gym. For example, in the sensory gym he can be a flying trapeze artist. At home, the parents should do three twenty-minute Floortime sessions every day with William. Get siblings involved, too, with each taking turns being the leader and the others have to follow his/her lead. The TV time should be limited to a maximum of an hour per day during the week, and one hour on weekends. Someone should be interacting with William all the time.

Now is the time to cue into his interactions. He's the boss of the Floortime. You ask his permission to join his play and try to get more circles of communication going and you will see his progress increase more rapidly. Transition, aggression and impulsivity will all improve when you do the things I have suggested to improve his program. He has good potential and I like what I'm hearing. I cannot wait to hear about his good progress in the near future.

### Rebecca School's response to Dr. Greenspan's suggestions

The recommendations made perfect sense to the team, however implementing them caused some apprehension. In working with William it is difficult to imagine where one might find a quiet enough space to do a Floortime session with him. He often looks totally overwhelmed by all the sounds and sights coming at his sensory system, and the Rebecca School is a rowdy place. Little William usually has his fingers plugging his ears and hovering over his eyes, trying to block out at least some of the stimulation. As a coping strategy William sticks to what he knows through memorization. In the mornings he comes in, hangs up his coat, puts away his backpack, comes into the classroom, then goes back out to his cubby, taking out his backpack and getting his lunchbox from it, then putting it back in, coming back to class and setting up his breakfast. Undress—check, put stuff away—check, eat breakfast—check . . . oh, wait, not check—no lunchbox. Despite doing everything independently and looking self-sufficient, William is precise in his sequence of the morning routine, as it is memorized. He is not thinking about or visualizing the fact that he will be eating breakfast in the next several minutes, and then adapting his behavior to a situation that he can predict. It seems to the classroom teacher that he does these actions when he is not even hungry. He first pours his protein drink from his thermos to the sippy cup, sometimes drinking it, other times not touching it the entire day. He then tries to throw out the thermos, in his attempt to clean up after himself (another step of the eating routine that he has memorized), and the TA's either fish it out of the garbage or tell him that it doesn't go in the garbage; he then puts it back in the lunchbox. He then takes out his applesauce, says, "Spoon, spoon, spoon," and eats that with a plastic spoon, which he then attempts to put back in his lunchbox. Corrected again, he complies, but he does the same thing the following day. He then eats his crackers, then the toast with butter, leaving all the crusts behind. Interrupting this routine results in anxious screaming, so letting him be the boss, seemed for a long time like the only option.

After hearing Dr. Greenspan's recommendations, the team decided that they would try breaking into William's routine by being playful with an emphasis on pretend play, in an effort to help him become more flexible. At first, he would only share the toast crust with a dinosaur puppet. Since William does not like the crust, giving it to the dinosaur posed no threat. As he developed a sense of safety and a sense of humor around this play scene, he began giving the dinosaur a bite of everything he ate before taking a bite himself. This of course did not happen in one day, but the morning routine became less rigid, more interactive, and consequently took longer. Luckily, the teacher did not concern herself with starting the morning greeting circle on time, so taking a long breakfast with dinosaurs was just fine. In fact, William became the boss of the morning circle. Often, when he became particularly excited by the dinosaur's distaste for some foods, which he spit out angrily or knocked out of William's hand, William would get up and do a tapping gallop around the room. One day the teacher mimicked William's tap and asked, "Oh, are we tap dancing now?" Not sure of what exactly had happened or what she meant, but sure of the fact that he liked the attention, William cautiously tapped a bit more. So did the teacher. She motioned for the TAs in the class to join. William ran over and crashed into the beanbag chair face down, only to look up a few seconds later to find all the adults in the room sitting on the floor, sighing and saying how tired they were from all the dancing. Not believing his good luck, William let out a roar of giggles and leaped up to tap dance some more. With some encouragement other kids in the class either joined the dance, sat and watched, shouting, "Dance, dance," every time the tapping stopped, following William's lead, or banged on the tambourine providing musical accompaniment to the dancing troupe.

This went on for twenty minutes. William felt so empowered and proud that he forgot all about the breakfast. The following day he came in, set the table, took a bite of food and got on the classroom dance floor. The most amazing thing, however, is that prior to making the first tap, he looked around to see if the others were paying attention—he was not about to dance without an audience and people that would follow him. He was thinking ahead, awaiting his groupies. The teacher said, "I think William is ready to tap. Here we go!"

## Chapter 12

# A Symphony of Fans

Flicking, looking, modifying his visual world in every way you can with just two hands, a toy, and New York's vertical landscape, Matthew transverses the world. With a head tilt and a curious upward glance, his perception of the world is very different from ours. He is intently focused on the details of the world he manipulates, and in that focus is able to manage his environment, internal as well as external. Scratch the surface, and you find an intensely talented, musical, funny boy. It takes some time and effort, but it's an effort that is amply rewarded.

I singlehandedly made it impossible for Matthew's mother to spend her fifteen minutes "playing and having fun" with Matthew when they came in for the admission interview. I did this by having among the toys that I offered them, an Elmo Phone. I don't know if you are familiar with this toy, but if you are a particular kind of kid, attracted to Sesame Street and to flashing electronic toys, it is an all but irresistible trap, and that's exactly what it was to Matthew. (Thankfully, a later child freed me of the phone by throwing it out an eighth floor window!) But Matthew became absorbed in the phone with its flashing and singing, "La, la, la, la—La, la, la, la, Elmo's Song" over and over again. Mom was really frustrated that Matthew couldn't really show his true self, and that he was really a talented and bright, creative child. Fortunately for us, we were able to get past my early mistake, and Matthew has become an adored and integral part of the Rebecca School Community.

Mom reports, "I had a normal pregnancy. He did, we thought, very well. He started talking; he said his first word when he was eight months old (*book*). We realized at about fourteen months that he knew all his letters, and was hitting all his milestones on the late side, until he wasn't walking, he took about three steps at sixteen months old, and then he just didn't walk anymore, and so I told my pediatrician that I wanted to have him evaluated. He was saying to wait to eighteen months, but I wanted to have him evaluated. So, I took him to a physical therapist who said that his issue wasn't a physical one but a sensory one. We added in around that time occupational and speech therapists, and a home educator. We had him evaluated by a neurologist who said he had PDD NOS. He was still talking at two, but he was identifying things with words, he would put two words together, but he wasn't saying things like, 'That smells,' or 'I love my dog.' That kind of thing. He wasn't saying things like that."

At eighteen months, Mom felt that "he was related, but when we had him evaluated, they said that his eye contact wasn't what it should be. Around two he started doing some stimming behaviors, flapping his hands a little bit, things like that. I remember that he used to stand like a tripod, on his head and two feet, a lot, and play like that, which we thought was strange. Before we had him evaluated for some reason I would go to the pediatrician and say, 'I think he's on the Autism Spectrum.' And he would say, 'No, he's related, he has eye contact, he has language, he's hitting his milestones; he's fine.' And then it turned out that he wasn't."

"So we had him in all these therapies. And we took him to a very well-known New York City pediatrician, and she told us to put him in forty hours of ABA therapy. I just couldn't imagine a two-year-old sitting for forty hours of ABA a week." Matthew went to a special-education pre-school, where he got a behaviorally based program, then onto a school for children with learning disabilities. "We stopped ABA altogether. We didn't feel it worked for him. He'd script a lot. He didn't like it. He didn't seem happy. His ABA therapist would come to the house and he would say, 'HI MARY, MY NAME IS MATTHEW, I LIVE AT 816 WEST 28TH STREET MY NUMBER IS 2125551212 MY HAIR IS BROWN MY EYES ARE BROWN . . .' He would just spew out her whole part so he could get to the playing part. It just didn't seem like it was generalizing. Three years ago my husband and I went to Son-Rise, and we started doing a Son-Rise program with him at home. When we went to Son-Rise and came home and started following his lead, I found that it was great. And it made him really happy, and he's been doing great since then. He's more and more related, he's much more joyful; since he's been at Rebecca we've seen that too. Since January he's beginning to read a little bit."

"He seems like a sensory kid to me. He's really into spinning things. He's really into fans." Dad jumps in. "He knows where every fan in Manhattan is. On the first, second, or third floors, if he's seen it once he remembers where it is."

Mom continues, "But we are also now able to have conversations with him about the fans. Whether they are off, whether they are on; isn't that great whether it's off or on. How fast is it going, fast or slow, faster than yesterday but slower than the day before. He'll say, 'Mommy look, the fan is on. It's going faster.' And the next day he'll say, 'Mommy Look. The fan is slower.' Or there's one fan on and two fans off. Or sometimes we'll count, on a certain stretch of Broadway maybe there's lots of fans, and he'll say, 'Count the ones that are on.' Then he'll say, 'Hurray!' at the end. But it's an interactive thing where we're really enjoying ourselves together." When asked if Matthew could answer why he liked one fan better than another, Mom replied that she did not think he could answer that question. "He doesn't answer 'Why' questions." Dad agreed.

The teachers note that while he has intense interests in things, like fans, he appears to be happiest when engaged, but that getting engaged with him is pretty difficult. It might begin with exact mirroring of what he is doing. "So he might begin playing with a wooden letter," says John, one of Matthew's teachers, "an 'M,' and he'll say, 'OOO, EEE, AHAH!'

and if you smile he'll be happy, but if not, he'll say, 'All done *OOO, EEE, AHAH!*' But if you get it going it becomes a back-and-forth, where he will touch the "m" and you say, '*OOO, EEE, AHAH*.' And if this gets going right it can go on for like an hour. But sometimes it is really difficult to engage him, sometimes he gets dysregulated. For instance, sometimes he'll do this thing where he picks a stuffed animal, and he spins it up in the air, labels it, and beats on it. So he'll say, 'Green Bear, spinning up in the air,' and he'll toss it up, and then bring it down and beat on it. If you try to engage, he is very, very resistant to that. If you say, '*WEEEE,*' when the monkey is up in the air he'll say, 'All done, *WEEEE*.' If you sit within three feet of him he'll say, 'Hands off, Hands off.' He's got really strong visual-spatial skills, so he knows exactly what you are doing all the time."

"He has expressed anger in certain ways," John says. "There were certain toys that he loved so much that they inhibited interaction, so we had to take them away. So, every time we did that, I would sit him down and say, 'I'm sorry, Matthew, but the Oscar toy is all done.' And, there have been a number of toys I've had to do that with, so when he's feeling angry at me he'll sit and say, 'Oscar toy's finished, blue toy's finished, purple toy's finished;' he'll sit there and list all the toys I've taken away. And, he never asked for the Oscar toy again."

Another of his teachers reminds us that Matthew has made progress in this area, and has been able to get angry, and repair from that anger much more often than he previously could. He is able now to get dysregulated, get involved in some visual stimulation, and recover from it. Sometimes he needs adult support for this, but sometimes he is able to actually do this on his own. When he first entered the school, he would get agitated, and then he would give the adults near him an impossible task that they would have to accomplish. The Teacher says, "He'd want you to say a word backwards. 'Say tomorrow backwards!' And he would give you something impossible that you could not do, and when you would fail at it, inevitably, he would respond by completely breaking down, and it would take a long time for him to repair. And now, what's happening is he might say, 'Say tomorrow backwards,' but when you tell him that you can't do it, he might cry and have that natural emotion, and he can repair from that in a way that is more like a typical kid his age." Now, he sets up those impossible situations so that he can be in an emotional relationship with the adult. This is in stark contrast to the essentially self-involved rituals he had previously used to try to help regulate himself.

### Sensory and Motor Strengths and Challenges as Understood and Described by the Rebecca School Staff

*Visual Spatial:*

- Strong visual-spatial processing, with a strong visual memory.

*Auditory:*

- Auditory sensitivities.

*Proprioceptive:*

- Proprioceptive input is regulating.

*Vestibular:*

- Vestibular work is regulating, but he tends to get upregulated quickly with vestibular work alone.
- OT recommends introducing vestibular input first, and then pairing it with proprioceptive work.

*Tactile:*

- Tactilely defensive, as he resists working with certain materials.

### Motor Processing and Planning:

- A challenge for him.
- Has trouble climbing, indicating some gravitational insecurity.
- Poor balance reactions.

## Rebecca School Program in Place Before Consulting with Dr. Greenspan

*Floortime: 4 x 20 min./day, Individual, in the classroom, with teacher, primarily.*

- Focus on Levels IV, V, and VI, as the teachers feel that the best way to help Matthew is to become more at ease, less anxious, and be better able to manage his world.

*Speech: 5 x 30 min./week, Individual.*

- Therapist addresses his shorter verbal communications in an effort to make his phrases into longer sentences.

*OT: 3 x 30 min./week, Individual.*

- Most sessions take place in the sensory gym to help him regulate his sensory system to support his communication. He gets some of his best continuous flow interactions while on a swing in the sensory gym. In sensory-based fantasy play, Matthew is capable of thirty to forty circles of communication, as opposed to ten to fifteen in other situations.

*Music Therapy: 1 x 30 min./week.*

- Very musical, perfect pitch, back and forth in a continuous co-regulated flow.

**Art Therapy: 2 x 20 min./week, with entire class.**

- Focus on peer interactions, with adult support. Work on building a therapeutic relationship.

### Dr. Greenspan's Recommendations

Matthew is eight-and-a-half years old, and has been attending the Rebecca School since the beginning of the school. He was diagnosed as having PDD-NOS at twenty-three months. Also notable in his story is that he was an early talker with a very good verbal memory, but was labeling. Initially, he had ABA and Son-Rise, and attended other schools before Rebecca School.

Matthew can focus and attend and has a good visual and auditory memory, but has a narrow range of interests and can get dysregulated when you try to broaden this. He is very likable; everyone loves him and he can be close to people, but he can also get fixed in rigid patterns or be dysregulated if you approach him in a way he doesn't want you to. We want to see him take more initiative in engaging with others. He can open and close circles of communication, but not across a broad range of themes. We want to have thirty to forty circles across a broad range of interests.

Matthew can do shared, social problem solving and can be quite sophisticated using his visual and auditory memory, but we want to broaden this and get it more flexible—broaden his emotional and intellectual range. He can use ideas and is beginning to use them in pretend play and can hold a little conversation, but we want to broaden this. We want to focus more on the pretend play to broaden his use of ideas in pretend play. We need to move further into more elaborate pretend play to help him become comfortable with a broader range of emotions.

Matthew can connect ideas together; answer "W" questions, but not "Why." He can respond to other people's ideas. We need to move to a more solid place with all "W" questions, especially "Why," so his memory is supported with logical thinking. Start off with things he is very interested in, like fans, and start asking a "Why" question and give multiple-choice help (good choice first, silly choice second), "Why do you want to see that fan? Because it's fun to look at or because you want to go to sleep?" I think he is ready for that and will do this quickly.

Then he is the type of child who can make good progress into multi-causal thinking and gray-area thinking. He will then become much more flexible.

### Constitutional and Maturational Variations

Matthew has a good auditory memory, but he lacks the pragmatic and social part. We have to help him use his language in a thinking-based way that will draw on his strong memory skills. Have questions and conversations focused on opinion-based conversations and imaginative play. It doesn't matter what the conversation is about, as long as it is dynamic and interactive. He does have some motor-planning challenges, but he also has some strengths in these areas because of his good memory. We want to expand his flexibility. Don't repeat climbing up a ladder the same way each day. Mix it up and help him to be creative and innovative.

Sensory modulation is an area in which Matthew has challenges. He sometimes is defensive in reaction to sensory input, and he is sometimes underreactive to similar input. This mixed reactivity makes it possible for him to get dysregulated very easily. We want to gradually expand his exposure to different kinds of sensory experiences and find ways to help him calm down. Music is a good way to help him. Playing instruments would be good.[1]

---

1  This is why we have interactive music therapists at the Rebecca School. We think it is an integral part of the program. In fact, inspired by Dr. Greenspan's feedback, Dr. John Carpente, Matthew's music therapist at the time, created an entire program using fans and interactive composition with Matthew as a way to get him "cooking."

Visual-spatial processing is a relative strength, and we want to help him become a good visual spatial thinker. He is a good candidate for *Thinking Goes to School*, two times a day for twenty-minute sessions at a minimum, for him to work on the different levels of visual spatial thinking.

Matthew's prognosis is best indicated by his learning curve over the next few months and years with an appropriate intervention program. As that curve continues on an upward trend, his prognosis for continued improvement will reflect that trend. Now that he is showing nice progress, we want to see if we can increase the flexibility, warmth, and engagement.

## Game Plan

I recommend that parents and others working with Matthew engage him in spontaneous interactive play, following his interests and pleasures, for eight twenty- to thirty-minute sessions each day. In these sessions, the parents can work on all the levels described above in imaginative play, or simple back-and-forth interactions around the things that interest him most. Challenge him to open and close as many circles of communication in a row as possible.

As a general rule, the healthiest pattern in a family would be for children to have their father a little bit every day, rather than all day Saturday and Sunday and none on the weekdays. The closer Matthew's family can come to this ideal, the better. Dad and Matthew should just have fun together, where Matthew is lit up and thrilled and delighted, and both are having fun. To do that, a child has to spend a lot of time with the adult, who has to be a regular part of his life. The stresses of modern life make this difficult sometimes, but I am pleased to see how hard Matthew's father has worked to make this a reality.

When the siblings are playing together for an hour, each one can be the leader for twenty minutes in a game where they are interacting with each other. Create a game that would be of interest to both of them and where they have to interact and collaborate in order to play. When Dad comes home, you can include Dad; he can play with each child alone or together.

### Program Responses to Dr. Greenspan's Recommendations

More one-on-one Floortime; at least five or six, twenty-minute sessions with focus on imaginative play. Use sensory support as needed. Join him. Work on his natural interests and then help him expand by meeting his goals more. He does not need to be obstructed, but you need to meet his interests in more flexible ways. Join him in meeting his goals. Use the fans in imaginative ways, animate the fan. Assume that the self-stimulatory interests really have a legitimate basis, something that gives him joy and pleasure. He may actually experience music when he sees the fans. Other individuals with processing problems who have a very good memory and good cognitive skills, may experience music when they see interesting sights and vice versa. Their minds work in different ways than our ways, but we don't know. We want to play off of that and assume that he has a good reason for liking fans and eventually he will tell us how rich his experience is. Instead of challenging and redirecting him, say, "Oh that looks exciting and fun." Have materials where you could build fans. Approach the person where their passion is. With Matthew, it's fans. Then it's not challenging versus joining, you are always joining and that's the key.

Broaden his sensory regulatory experiences using music and other activities for self-calming. He should have peer play opportunities every day with a child at school, a child, who is at least as verbal as Matthew, and as interactive. Anything that increases engagement and interaction is good, and anything that decreases interaction and engagement should be stopped.

The ticket is joy, happiness, and constantly expanding.

*Chapter 13*

# I Love You, Now Leave Me Alone

Bright, quick, and lost in a world dominated by his hands as he rubbed them, squeezed them together, and looked intently at them, David drifted into his admission interview in the company of both parents. He was anxious, nervous in a new and confusing space, but engaging and able to light up with a smile as he made a loud squeal that sounded to me like joy. Even in his self-absorption he was charming from the start, and it is this charm that endears him to those around him. Everyone loves him; and this lovely child receives the kind attention of those around him. David has the dazed look of someone not quite sure where he is or what is expected of him under most circumstances. But when you catch him, when you catch the spark, he lights up and talks to you in a lilting voice of the delighted boy he can be.

His mother says that, "Even from the start he was low toned. A little after a year we started physical therapy. At eighteen months they thought it was apraxia of speech, so we started getting speech therapy, and all the therapies with early intervention." But even with intensive early intervention, David began to have additional symptoms around the age of four. "We started to see some odd behaviors, like the stimming started. At that point he was very social." David was being followed by a prominent New York developmental pediatrician at this time. He was diagnosed at that point with PDD, and his parents were told that he was on the spectrum. He had, "spectrum-like qualities, although he displayed certain characteristics that were not so spectrum-like." He was in a typical preschool for a year, and got ABA after school, and then David spent a year in a school that combines the ABA approach with the DIR approach, and then he came to Rebecca School.

Mom feels, "that he made the most progress up to the age of four or so, before the stimming started. Then he started showing more of these self-stimulatory behaviors, he started getting lost in his own world, less always on, you know?" In answer to a question about what kind of treatment David was receiving at this time, Mom responded, "That's when we really started getting heavy duty ABA. I don't know if it's a correlation, but . . . we started at the age of five to get ABA and more intense therapies. One-on-one, and you know he was making progress, but his behaviors really . . . his play skills were never that great. He always had motor-planning issues, he never really loved toys. He loves people more than toys. He loves reading a book with me, he loves being roughhoused, he likes physical activities like swinging. He's not the kind of kid who is going to sit on the floor and build blocks and Legos. I mean, he was taught all those things so he is able to do it, but he would never pick up the blocks on his own because he really doesn't love doing that kind of thing."

PROMPT therapy[1] helped him with his apraxia, and at this point, at eight, "He is able to tell us what he wants, answer our 'Who' questions, "What" questions, but he's not conversational. He doesn't initiate so often; he answers questions. He can talk in sentences, but we thought it would be more by now considering the progress he made from four to five. His biggest problem is that he has these self-stimulatory behaviors that are so reinforcing for him that when he is doing them he doesn't show us what he's capable of. He looks at his hands, moves his hands, squeezes his hands, and he also sometimes scripts, like videos, books that he reads; it's like he gets lost in a little script."

During his intake screening, David and his Dad had trouble playing with dolls and trucks, and things that you could build a story around. It was clear that these were not the kind of toys that David wanted to play with. When

---

1   PROMPT is a kind of speech therapy. The PROMPT Institute has its own website, and I refer you there to learn more about this therapy.

he sat with these toys he was not engaged with his father, did not seek out contact with words or with his body, and spent a lot of time occupied with his hands. More physical, sensory toys were equally unsuccessful. David was able to answer questions about the toys, color, number, what they were if he recognized them, but never answered a "Why" question and never initiated an interaction. He was perfectly calm, but disengaged, and was interested in me and the camera, looking up quizzically on several different occasions. When the fifteen-minute playtime was up, and Dad went with Mom to speak to the Rebecca School's director, I got a chance to play.

With a sense of David's processing issues and motor-planning problems, I tried to use blankets and fabrics to find if I could tap into David's interests. None of the more sedate games worked, so I invited David out into an open space with me to play catch. His motor-planning issues definitely interfered, he was afraid to get hit by a ball that he knew he couldn't catch, but he was willing to take the ball from me, and with a lot of over-the-top affect and anticipatory encouragement, "One……….. Two…………THREE!" he was able to go back and forth in a purposeful and engaged way. I was careful to allow him to have his hands as solace, and he showed me that he needed to walk away from me and circle around before he could come back after a throw to me, but he stayed engaged. Then we moved to a big beanbag chair. This big, overstuffed velour beanbag chair was attracting him, but he was afraid to move close. I called, in my most enticing and reassuring voice to him, and he wanted to come, but was evidently overwhelmed with the notion of coming up to the chair that was going to give him so much sensory feedback at once. Finally, after about five minutes, and several approaches and retreats, he came and sat on the chair next to me for the briefest of seconds, then jumped up squealing, evidently very happy with himself. I knew that there was a lot to David, but that his motor issues, his sensory-processing issues and his anxiety, were going to be obstacles for him to overcome.

The classroom teacher reports that in class David is able to stay calm and regulated for most of the time, and that he will seek out some sensory comfort to calm down when he is overwhelmed. He can stay engaged, and talks more to adults than he will to other kids in the classroom. He gives the staff the impression that he wants to interact with the other kids, but that he doesn't know how to do it, even when supported by the staff. When he is really engaged and regulated, he can even do more complex problem solving, although these times are really inconsistent. They see that they get the best from David when he is involved in a sensory activity; for instance, the swing is a motivator for him.

David has a mixed sensory profile. He seeks out certain sensory input, while he gets overwhelmed easily by certain other types of sensory input. The occupational therapist feels that he is constantly trying to filter out sensory input that he finds overwhelming and confusing.

He loves to work with her, and loves to sing as he swings or bounces on a therapy ball. David also craves light touch, and so teachers in the classroom and the occupational therapist have developed tickling and squeezing games with him. They feel that during this time they are able to get their best back-and-forth co-regulated circles. However, these interactions still lack flexibility, and while he may be able to stay engaged for longer periods of time, he is not building upon the other person's ideas in a true collaboration.

### Sensory and Motor Strengths and Challenges as Understood and Described by the Rebecca School Staff

*Visual Spatial:*

- Wears glasses to correct vision, visual acuity not an issue.
- Cannot see the big picture, cannot put visual details into a larger context.
- Would not search systematically for a desired item. Would look in some small number of places where it had previously been.

*Auditory:*

- Easily overstimulated.

### Proprioceptive:

- Deep pressure and joint compression help to organize him and regulate him.
- Input helps him to motor plan.

### Vestibular:

- Enjoys swinging in a linear plane.

### Tactile:

- Enjoys light tickles or light massage.

### Feeding:

- Feeding continues to be an area of concern; if not given verbal and tactile prompts, David tends to take overly large bites and fill his mouth with food without chewing and swallowing appropriately.

### Motor Processing and Planning:

- Difficulty with gross- and fine-motor skills.
- Low overall tone.
- Weak core, inhibiting planning and execution.

## Rebecca School Program in Place Before Consulting with Dr. Greenspan

*Floortime: 4–6 x 20 min./day, Individual, in the classroom, with teacher or one specific teaching assistant, primarily.*

*Speech: 3 x 30 min./week, Individual.*

He has improved his receptive language since he came to Rebecca School, and is now working on prepositional language, like where things are in space. Although as his visual/spatial processing is challenged, he has difficulty with more complex ideas like "in front of." He has trouble with pronouns, and has trouble with more abstract concepts in general. He will now, however, walk into the classroom and seek the attention of a teacher he likes and say, "Good morning!" even if he is not prompted first. The SLP had worked all year on his oral-motor/articulation issues, and reports that now David is much more tolerant of her work with him around his mouth, and that he no longer drools as he did at the beginning of the year. She has worked hard with him to decrease overstuffing his mouth, and instead to chew and swallow his food.

### OT: 3 x 30 min./week, Individual.

- David's therapy sessions are conducted both in the sensory gym and in the classroom to work on regulation, motor planning, and fine-motor or ADL-based activities.
- A sensory diet that includes different tactile activities is being created by the therapist for use in the classroom to help arouse and engage David in the classroom activities.
- Motor-planning tasks are difficult for David to plan, initiate, and execute. When combined with proprioceptive-based movement activities, David is better prepared and more aroused to engage with his therapist in the motor-planning activity.
- His therapist is introducing different sensory-based hand strengthening exercises to increase his fine-motor control and different proprioceptive activities to strengthen his trunk and core muscles for seated tasks.

### PT: 2 x 30 min./week, Individual.

- Working to improve dynamic balance skills, while maintaining attention and engagement, to allow for fluid ambulation during transitions.
- Working to improve strength and coordination, with sustained mutual engagement, to allow for increased participation in physical tasks and activities with his peer group.

*Music Therapy: 1 x 30 min./week.*

*Art Therapy: 2 x 20 min./week, with two peers.*

## Dr. Greenspan's Recommendations

David is about eight-and-a-half years old, and has been diagnosed with PDD. He has always been very social and is very social to this day. He has had more intensive ABA work, and still gets a little bit now, even though he is now at the Rebecca School. He can focus and attend, but you can lose him when he gets frustrated or overloaded with sensory input. Everyone has been contributing to that by treating the lack of focus and the absorption in his hands or scripts as a negative, rather than as another avenue of opportunity. He can engage and is warm and everyone likes and loves him. His strong social capacities continue, but are not consistent because he's not initiating as much as we would like to see, and we here and at home have not yet come up with a consistent approach to help with the self-stimming and scripting.

David can open and close circles of communication, but is not consistent in getting a continuous flow. He's dependent on our providing the initiative. He can problem solve, but initiative is not strong enough and he depends on us. We are inadvertently continuing that behavior. David can use ideas and has a good vocabulary, but hasn't gotten into pretend play.

There are vulnerabilities at Milestones III, IV, and V that are limiting his higher-level thinking capacities. We will continue to be frustrated unless we help him master these fundamental building blocks. For a child who has a lot of potential like David, it is imperative to develop these early building blocks, or else he will suffer the consequences of having more limited progress than is optimal. David can connect ideas together and sometimes answer "Why" questions, often with multiple-choice help.

## Constitutional and Maturational Variations

David has auditory-processing and language challenges. In terms of motor planning, he has a history of low-muscle tone and sequencing challenges. He is sensory overreactive, but his visual spatial is an area that we can strengthen further so he will be more big-picture oriented.

## Game Plan

The program now is an excellent one, but the focus should now be on my recommendations to improve the program. Remember that you get what you practice—if you practice his taking the initiative five percent of the time, and do for him ninety-five percent of the time, then that is you will get.

Work on initiative, imagination, and entering his world of scripts and self-stimulation and make it a constructive, interactive, initiative-taking experience. To help him take more initiative, we have to create settings where he's motivated to take initiative. Create a sensory environment with things he likes, but let him pick what he wants to do there. If he starts stimming, join him. Have Clifford stim with him. This is one of the most subtle and hard things for even the most experienced professionals to get, how to harness the child's initiative. We're intimidated by the self-stimulatory or perseverative behaviors. Be very playful with him. Make sure he takes the initiative two-thirds of the time. If he runs away, play a chase game. Whatever he does we interpret as him taking the initiative and join him. We don't want to frighten or make it painful for him. We want it to be very pleasurable and enjoyable.

Make different assumptions about his stimming. Assume the child is doing this automatically and doesn't want to do it or that he loves to do it and it's a secret passion or the child loves to do it because it creates music or interesting sensory experiences that we can't understand. For a verbal child like David, what we want to do (and this may take a month or two to find out) is, using very positive affect and approval (use your natural curiosity), to move our hands with him and ask him what happens when we do that? What kind of experience does he have? Give him multiple-choice options. Eventually, we can get a full and rich description of this behavior and then he can tell us what the experience is like and tell us "I need your help to stop doing it" or he may tell us "I need you to do it with me." But I want you to enter his self-stimulatory world, make it interactive and sometimes distract him to something else and ask him if he liked it when you switch from hand games to reading or what would he rather do: look at his hands or read? Sometimes you can even start doing it before he does and say, "Look at me. Look at what I'm doing." Turn the self-stimming into interactive games. It's kind of like Daddy engaging Mommy in her most peculiar habits. We all appreciate it when our loved ones indulge us in our idiosyncrasies.

Self-stimming can become a basis for pretending. You can be orchestra leaders. Make this as imaginative as possible. I don't care if he scripts. That can be the first line of a new drama. Once he says a line in a script, it's okay as long as you don't script back from the same drama, and play off his script. When he is scripting and it's not relevant to what's going on, join him in the script and begin pretending. I'd like to see a little more time spent on one-on-one and initiative taking, eight times a day with different therapists working with him twenty minutes or more. He needs lots of time at home working on his initiative, as well. The ABA should be focused only on these things that don't require initiative, like teaching a skill that is okay if he just memorizes it.

At the school I get the feeling that the staff has given up on imaginative play. As he takes more initiative I want you, in the sensory environment or wherever he is at his best, to start doing some dress up using costumes and try to get into some imagination. If you can't right away, don't worry about it and keep working on initiative. Treat every behavior as an opportunity for some pretending and trying to discover what's fun about his stimming activities.

We want to create a favorable sensory environment, both at home and at school. It's not in his interest to be in a noisy environment. He should be taken out of such environments as often as necessary. I'd do a lot of music and rhythmic activities with him throughout the day. At the same time as you are doing this, try to get a continuous flow and a lot of language.

The fear of losing him is the ticket to actually losing him. It undermines encouraging him to take initiative.

Let's start with the staff doing this joining with him on the self-stimming. Parents can come in once a week and observe how they do it and do it with them and give them some tips like not to do it at home until they are more comfortable.

### Rebecca School's Response to Dr. Greenspan's Recommendations

We received the above suggestions from Dr. Greenspan, and then we had to put them into action. Following this case, I met with the classroom staff to debrief around Dr. Greenspan's suggestions. They were concerned that they had been described as "giving up" and were having trouble hearing that they in fact were doing well with David. They were having trouble seeing how they could make this good program even better. I reassured the truly talented head teacher and her teaching assistants that they were doing a great job with David, and helped them understand how they could go even farther in getting him to take the initiative. I walked away from this meeting unconvinced that I had any impact, and convinced that they were going to have a hard time implementing the suggested revisions. But, as is so often the case, I had vastly underestimated the considerable strength and flexibility of the Rebecca School staff, because the next day the following took place.

There was a morning meeting where the students and staff in David's room gathered to get warmed up. The teacher offered each child a chance to sing and play a drum, while everyone else, students and staff, followed his or her lead. It was really a remarkable example of how this team really took it to heart that students need to be supported in taking initiative. One student followed another as they sang, sometimes made up words, and all of the other students and staff sang along. There was real joy at the table. Then, it was David's turn. He started with the drum, but then put it down and began rubbing his hands together. Everyone stared at him, and the head teacher tried to get him to use the drum. He rebuffed her, and looked at his hands, and continued to rub them. Then, in a moment so clear that it was impossible to miss, I saw the light go on over the teacher's head, and she looked around the table and said, "Let's do what David's doing!" She nodded at everyone, and the table got silent, as everyone rubbed their hands together in imitation of David, and looked at them. It was very quiet, and the uncommon silence prompted David to look up. When he saw everyone imitating him, he sat quietly for a moment, and burst out with a squeal of joy, which of course, the entire table imitated. Shocked, he went back to the intense focus on his hands, and so did his tablemates. The silence again got David to look up, and when he did, he was greeted with the sight of a table full of adults and children rubbing their hands together and staring at them. He let out another squeal, and then, for several minutes he led the group. He showed them how to rub their hands together and intently stare at them in just the right way, then he shared his intense joy and excitement in his laughter and squealing, which, of course, they echoed. Back and forth they went in this true dialogue of joy and understanding. For David and this class, this was a breakthrough moment.

But, the home program is always a concern, and particularly so with this instruction to follow this behavior in David. Mom had spent so many years fighting, trying to extinguish, this hand-wringing and staring in her son. In the case conference she said that all of his functioning had deteriorated at the same time that he got absorbed in his hands. It did not seem likely to me that she would be able to take the chance and follow David's lead on this much-hated behavior? That night, the head teacher in the class got the following e-mail from David's mother:

*Hi, Sara,*

*I got your note today about how David is responding to our new method of working with him. I am glad to hear that you think he is responding well to your joining him. I wanted to write you and let you know how our experiences are going as well. Although Greenspan said to wait and see how he's doing at school first, I decided to go ahead and try some of his suggestions at home a little as well. I am really having some great interactions with David. Like you, I will begin to interact with him by joining his train of thought or activity and then almost immediately, he looks at me and we begin having a back and forth flow of communication.*

*For example, tonight he was scripting something about Clifford and I jumped in and started to talk about Clifford with a lot of affect, he then looked at me and said, "You are silly." We then started to do silly things and sing silly songs. This then led into suppertime where he helped me cook dinner, and we talked about our favorite foods. We had a sustained interaction for a good half an hour. We probably could have even continued longer. It was probably the best session we've had in a long time. It seems so far that not fighting the stimming and joining it may be an important piece of the puzzle for David.*

*I also got his brother to copy him when he was acting silly last night. David looked at Michael and went over to him and gave him a hug. He was soo happy that he was playing with him with his rules.*

*I just wanted to let you know what was happening here. Keep me posted about how things are going at school.*

*Thanks,*

*David's Mom*

Now, David is the king of the school. There is no one who does not know him, indeed, there is no one who is not totally charmed and in love with him! To follow David down the hall is to look into the smiling welcoming faces of all who come toward him. He has a knack for engaging people. He relies on the adoring and affectionate look, and laughter, and phrases, like a giggling, spirited, "I love you," when in an interaction he finds difficult. I had the great pleasure of watching his speech therapist, Jen, who is so clearly fond of him, and who is one of the greatest Floortimers I know, work with David in the hallway recently. As she pushed and prodded him to connect his ideas, and to think, he was as cute and disarming as any child could possibly be. He laughed and leaned in for a hug, he wanted to be tickled, and he even pulled out the "I love you!" Jen turned to me briefly with a face that said, "I'm melting!" Then she turned back to him and continued to push him to stay in the interaction, to follow his ideas through to some conclusion, and to think, think, think!

This seems to me to be one of the key ways in which the program has changed for David, and for all of the children at the school. We have gotten better at not being seduced by the charm and beauty of the children, and at continuing to push them to grow, continuing to push them up the developmental ladder, all while giving them time to think. This has become one of the themes of the school, "Thinking is work," and we have tried to implement it wherever we can. We have tried to disengage from the notion that we need to achieve some goal, and we try to support therapists and teachers alike as they slow down, leave space and allow the children to think and process at their own rates.

We noticed that the entire school seemed to have paused at the Functional Emotional Developmental Milestone IV.V. We were really good at helping children to stay regulated and available for interaction, and we got good at really helping children to get engaged with us. We learned to support back-and-forth interactions, and scaffolded children as they did emotionally meaningful back and forths in emotionally meaningful problem-solving interactions. And then kids stopped. We did considerable soul-searching about this. We consulted with the experts, and I talked with Dr. Greenspan at length, over months. Finally, sitting with the Floortime team, we realized that what the first four FEDMs had in common was that they required the staff to insert themselves. They allowed talented, enthusiastic people to jump in and interact in an addition sort of way. What FEDM V required was that the child begin to develop symbols in his or her head, and the skill and the enthusiasm of the staff did not match up with what was needed. They liked to fill the space with their enthusiasm and desire to help; FEDM V was going to require that they leave space and time.

Once we realized this as a Floortime team, we were ready to help the school see it as well, and we had our work cut out for us. We began to show video during our weekly staff training of us allowing processing and "thinking" time in our work with the kids. One of our team members, Elizabeth, invented the notion of "FloorMIME"—that's Floortime but with an emphasis on silence. We permeated the school, a gang of mimes (a frightening image), leaving space so that the kids could do the work.

So, this is one primary way that the program has changed, in general, since the time of David's initial conference. We now allow time for these kids to express their individual processing differences in the work. The pace has slowed down, and this has allowed the kids, and particularly kids like David, to speed up!

## Chapter 14

# A Vantage, or an Exit?

"There's nothing here I really like." Luke was looking for Legos.
"You could play with these," I said pointing to a bin of toys. I brought out for him and his mother to play with.

"No," he said hesitantly, not particularly defiantly. He was sure that he and his mother would have absolutely nothing to say about the things in the basket; he had no interest in them.

"Well, you could play with these things." I brought out another bin. He and his mother just stared. They looked at each other. Mom reached into her purse and pulled out the Legos, tiny meticulous robot-part Legos, and Luke squatted on the floor as his Mom looked on with a calm admiring. I watched as he carefully put tiny piece after piece on his minute creation, and it slowly evolved into a human-like creature. I got a chance to step in to play, and asked him about his robot.

"Well, these are its legs."

"Do you think we can make it stand," I asked? We tried. There was no way that its tiny feet would hold it up. "Maybe we could make it kneel." Luke complied, and the robot could kneel. Luke fiddled with a piece he was having trouble getting onto his robot. "Maybe we could use another piece and make it into something else?"

"No," he said thoughtfully, but with a finality that left no question about what he wanted to do.

"What is it I can tell you that can be helpful?" In only the fourth month of the Rebecca School, Luke's Dad wants to fill in Luke's developmental history on the phone with Dr. Greenspan, but he doesn't know where to start. With some prompting, he begins. "He was a child who did not particularly care for being held. He would seek out your lap and sit in it, but he would not return an embrace, or particularly care to return an embrace. He met most of his milestones, most of them on the early side, but when he crawled, he dragged one leg. We reported this to our pediatrician, but he was, well, he simply failed us, he did not lead us in a direction that would lead us to figure things out, he simply sort of noted it, and let it pass by, although it strikes me as a notable development at the time.

"At the age of about two-and-a-half or three, when other of our friends who had children this age would wax sort of sentimental about having another, my wife and I would look at each other and think, 'Why are we not feeling about Luke this way?' To us the experience of raising such a child seemed fraught with complications, difficulty, and labor. At three he went to school, and the single thing we noticed was he preferred to do things on his own rather to take part with any group. If he wanted to use a particular toy, he would wait until the other kids were finished with it, and then he would run over and get it, even if the kids were being summoned then to sit down and have juice. He didn't fit in with any of the other kids. He seemed, at the end of each day, it was only a half day then, he would flop down on the floor when he saw you, as if he was utterly, had been, sort of applied every bit of energy in his reserve to get through that morning, and he was now falling apart. He had a teacher in that class, an apprentice, who was very bright, and very fond of Luke, and very interested in him. He was really scapegoated at this school, his experience was awful. The head teacher, even if her back was turned to the class and she had no idea of who could have been responsible for a particular incident, would turn around and say, 'Luke!' And, it was very unfortunate for him. But, at one point I was saying to this young woman, 'You know, I'm kind of proud of Luke because he seems to be different from the other boys around him who seem plotting and conniving and secretive. Luke, when he has a problem with somebody, he deals with it right then. If someone takes a toy from him, he grabs it right back. He doesn't do what the other kids do, look around, see if anyone is watching, then smack the kid when no one is looking, and grab the toy. They've figured out how not to get caught, and I don't think that is a very admirable quality.' And this young woman, who was very fond of Luke, grew thoughtful for a moment, and said, 'Yes, and you wonder why Luke hasn't figured out how not to get caught either?' And that was the first moment, up until then my wife and I had always thought we had a very engaging, very eccentric, very complicated and difficult child, but. . . .

"He was not easily comforted, he wasn't like another child. You couldn't just pick him up off the floor at six months or seven months and hold him tightly and soothe him and have him recover. The embrace seemed sometimes to even increase the agitation. He seemed eccentric, because he is a kind of prodigy as an artist. The very first thing we began to notice was all of his toys, he would disassemble, and put back together in new ways. As the youngest child that I can remember. You'd buy him a truck, he'd take it apart, he'd combine it with parts from another truck and make a new kind of truck, which he would then play with. He seemed, while not seeming astonishingly brilliant, he seemed very smart, very attentive, very interested. A very quirky and eccentric boy. Clearly interested in what he wanted to do. His inability to take part with the activities of other children, we saw as a decision to be independent. And at this point, he was always sort of charismatic around other kids. They always sort of wanted to do what he was doing, which made him seem to a greater degree individual. Of course, what I think now is that what they were trying to do was play with him, and he would not take part. At one point we were on a beach and Luke was doing something, and a little boy came up and wanted to play with Luke, and Luke picked up his toys and ran away down the beach. And my wife and I thought, *'This is Luke's problem in life. He's so charismatic that he is always doing these things, and other children want to do them, and Luke very sensibly, is saying 'No, I'm engaged in something that is a solitary pursuit.'* My wife and I both have solitary careers; to us this seemed like a very natural state of existence. I wouldn't think that now if I had a second child."

After the second year, Luke was asked not to come back. He went to a school for children with learning disabilities, where he was the only child in the class who could read, and became a behavior problem there. He left this school for a third school, where his experience varied really according to his relationship with the teacher of the classroom. His last three years were really difficult there, and as his behavior worsened, his parents put him on medication. "Everything under the sun, as attempts," Dad says. "Prozac disinhibited him, most of the stimulants made him very cranky, some of them tranquilized him overmuch, Risperdal gave him dystonia[1]. He ended up on Concerta, and a small dose of Risperdal with a small dose of Abilify to cover what the Risperdal wasn't covering. Since he has been at Rebecca, we have just about weaned him off all his medications." He was asked to leave this third school as well, and the parents brought him to Rebecca School because they felt, "that he's perfectly bright, and if he wishes to know the names of the nine justices of the Supreme Court he's capable of doing it. But nothing is going to matter if he can't at some point, by the age of eighteen have some independence in life. And we felt that Rebecca would offer that opportunity for him.

"He's quite engaged, quite easy to talk to, but he is quite voluble. He will talk for hours about the robot base, and what he's building for it and what they are doing. There is an element of empathic engagement in his talk now. I've heard him ask people how they are. 'Are you okay? Are you sad?' In ways that make me hopeful there is some quality there that can be enlarged. He can tell you why he is happy or sad. He's an adolescent, so sometimes he will say, 'Dad, don't ask me about that now.' He's deeply sensitive, very concerned when he feels other people are in pain or suffering in any way. He's oddly closeted within his own consciousness and yet, there do seem to be windows out of which he at least has a vantage if not, perhaps, an exit.

---

1  Dystonia is a neurologically based movement disorder. It is marked by muscle contractions that might cause repetitive movements and abnormal postures. It can be caused by some of the drugs prescribed for Luke.

"His artwork has progressed, 'Extravagantly.' As an artist I regard him more as a peer than as a student." Dad lights up. "He has taken on more and more complicated structures, his ambitions and intentions have been more complicated, the designs are more complicated. He loves to build with Legos, with clay, with various molding materials. He builds robot figures that are so lifelike and imaginative that you feel as if, out of the corner of your eye, you can almost see them move. Interestingly, I asked him if he would be willing to make a sculpture of me, and he didn't want to for the longest time, but he did, and finally he made the only really bland sculpture I have ever seen him make! If they're robots they are so vital, they really seem possessed of their own life."

"It's amazing to me that he can solve, and it really speaks to the disconnected neurology of his brain, but he can solve the most sophisticated technical problems having to do with incredibly complicated structures of cranes and robots. He uses Erector set parts. He never builds the device or the object that the kit was intended for. He always uses it in his own way. I once asked him how he does it, and he told me, 'I see them in my mind, and then I make them.' He can solve technical problems of true complexity, and yet, when he comes home at the end of the day, if the door of the apartment is closed, and he has things in his hands, he simply kicks at the door until I arrive. And no amount of my pointing out that, 'Luke, you could have put your things down on the floor, opened the door, and then picked them up,' will help. It will lead him to just lose his temper and say, 'What, did you want me to break everything that I own?!' He is an either/or sort of character. If he cannot do the thing that he wants, it means that you're telling him that permanently, for the rest of his existence, he will never be able to do it. He cannot see any shades of meaning or variation, or the possibility of, 'Oh yeah. I could just open the door, couldn't I?'

"Luke always needs an object," Dad continues, "during any period of transition. If we're going to go outside, if we're going to take a walk, if we are going to do any of these things, he insists on bringing with him, if you can finally persuade him to go outside which is not a small task, he will bring an object with him, a robot or a toy of some kind, and use it as a way to insulate him from the experience we are actually having. So when we are taking a walk, instead of actually taking a walk through the woods and paying attention to the birds or the trees, or the things I am pointing out to him, he will want to talk about what the robot is doing, if he is not complaining that the walk is too long! One of the things that we wonder is, is there a way to work that so that he could broaden his experience of life in some way instead of being shut out, or feeling that he has to defend himself. We wonder if there is a way that he could order his life in such a way that he can be open to more."

The classroom staff also sees his artistic side, but they have seen him become more flexible, and report that he has begun to make friends in the classroom, which is something that he was not doing in the beginning of the year. His anxiety throughout the day has decreased, although he still gets anxious at times in school. Transitions are difficult for him, and at times, he can get really dysregulated. He is very protective of his creations, and will get very upset if someone touches them or damages one of them. He can also get dysregulated during simple transitions. He can connect his ideas logically all the time, but at the beginning of the year this was not so. For example, recently he was upset, and when questioned he was able to say he was upset because his bus had broken down yesterday, and it had taken him a really long time to get home, and "Now, I'm still a little angry." Another time, he was upset because a teacher told him that he, the teacher, was leaving Rebecca School. When approached, he suggested that he build a scale to show how upset he was. On a scale of one to ten, he said that he was a one. The adult in the interactions pointed out to him that this implied he was no longer upset at all. He replied, "I'm a one on the outside, but I'm still a ten on the inside." He paused and thought. "I'm holding it in."

Dad added, "It's easier for me to see than maybe it is for people at the school, but I am pleased to see that he is changing in the ways the classroom staff describes, but I am also aware of how the atmosphere of the school allowed him to do this. At his old school the behavioral models were an agony for him. He would get right up to the minute when he was supposed to get his points, and something would happen and he would lose his control, and he would lose his points. He was miserable and unhappy and angry. He was very unhappy last spring and it got to the point where his mother and I began to wonder how much longer we could live with him as a practical matter, as he got older and bigger. And the change in him since he has begun at Rebecca is extraordinary, compared to where he was last spring. I know that he feels very safe. Parts of him that I feel intuitively he has kept under wraps, protected, undercover, all of his young life, practically, at least his public life in terms of education, are starting to relax and emerge. He's a very much more complete boy, human being, than he was six months ago, I think."

Dad sat quietly for a moment, and then spoke with great emotion. "The change in him . . . I was really worn out on him last spring, and I really started to think, because every day he came home and he'd be enraged! He'd have that hour-long bus ride where he'd been teased, and he'd be screaming! It would be a half-an-hour until he would calm down. And I thought, you know, I'm not sure if he gets this much bigger," Dad held his forefinger and his thumb slightly apart, "and suddenly, you know, um, I didn't know. This school has been, I wouldn't have imagined there was a possibility. I wouldn't have imagined, the child he is now I thought had disappeared. I really had thought it'd been eclipsed by adolescence, by hormonal things and complications in the world as it is. I had no idea that he could come back. And I think also getting rid of the drugs, he's not pacing as much, did you notice that, too? Since we've cut back on Ritalin he's really has slowed down. And the Abilify is gone now, as of today.

"Thank you, this has been a school from a dream. I really did not think I could have this life anymore. I thought I was going to have the life where you finally just, and his psychopharmacologist took me aside and said, 'Listen, you're not facing this, he's going to need a residential program,' and I couldn't bear it. Of course you can't. But I was also aware, well, there might come a point where I could bear it. This life is no longer possible; we couldn't do that. And that was probably true, but that went in another direction. I never thought that I could have back this child. I thought he was really gone. So, bless you all. It's an amazing story."

### Sensory and Motor Strengths and Challenges as Understood and Described by the Rebecca School Staff

*Visual Spatial:*

- Good visual acuity, although he has difficulty seeing the forest for the trees.

*Auditory:*

- Sensitive to loud screams and incessant chatter.

*Proprioceptive:*

- Will seek proprioceptive input when dysregulated, pacing, wall pushes, etc.

*Vestibular:*

- Avoids vestibular input.

*Tactile:*

- Tactile defensiveness.

*Oral-Motor:*

- Picky eater; eats plain pasta every day for lunch.
- Difficulty with articulation.

*Motor Processing and Planning:*

- Tends to be sedentary.
- Will sit on the sidelines rather than play group sports with peers.
- Delayed anticipatory reactions.
- Poor gross-motor bilateral coordination.

### Rebecca School Program in Place Before Consulting with Dr. Greenspan

*Floortime: 4–6 x 20 min./day, Individual, in the classroom, with teacher or one specific teaching assistant, primarily.*

- Can connect ideas logically most of the time. This is in contrast to him at the beginning of the year where he might have needed considerable support to answer the "Why" questions. Now he is able to answer open-ended "Why" questions consistently.

*Speech: 2 x 30 min./week, Individual, 1 x 30 min./week, group.*

- Work on articulation and oral-motor skills to improve his lateral emission of airflow for sounds.

*OT: 2 x 30 min./week, Individual.*

*Art Therapy: 2 x 20 min./week, with two peers.*

- After initial resistance to polymer sculpting medium, Luke has embraced it. Recently, he has begun placing his robots and other creations in environments, for instance, in a city, or beside a stream with shrubs, as opposed to the isolated creations he had previously insisted on making. Also recently, his robots have taken on more human characteristics.

### Dr. Greenspan's Recommendations

Luke, at thirteen years old, has many strengths. He has a history of having had very good memory capacities, but weaker motor- and sensory-modulation and social capacities. He would get dysregulated very easily and therefore was a challenge at school and at home, because when he would get dysregulated he found it hard to control his own behavior.

Luke can focus and attend, but doesn't have the emotional range and flexibility we would like to see. Within his interests of robots and his gifts and talents for sculpting and building things, particularly robots, he can be very focused. He can engage with real warmth, but again he doesn't show the range and depth we'd like to see in many situations. In particular, if he is frustrated or if things don't go his way he can become dysregulated, but will stay engaged. Luke can be purposeful and interactive and get into a continuous flow of interaction, but with limitations in the flexibility and range. He can also do shared, social problem solving. Here, too, we want to help him improve his range and flexibility.

Luke can use ideas and has creativity and imagination in many areas, particularly in spatial concepts and art, as it relates to the mechanics of building things and music. He is a little less verbal in terms of "writing the great novel" during imaginative play. We want to help him apply this to all the emotional ranges, like anger and frustration, as well as the things he is interested in.

Luke can be logical and answer all the "W" questions, including "Why" questions, and even give you multi-causal "Why" answers and occasionally do some gray-area thinking. However, for the most part Luke tends to be at the early stages of logical thinking and all-or-nothing thinker and hasn't advanced fully to gray-area thinking where he can see the shades and subtlety of a wide range of feelings. By age thirteen, we would hope that he could advance to reflective thinking where he can wonder why he feels differently than he usually does in a certain situation. This is a goal for him and is within his grasp once he masters a broader range of gray-area thinking, particularly around frustration, disappointment, and anger. So we want to move Luke more in gray-area thinking and expand his emotional range that he can apply logic to and help him become a reflective thinker.

## Constitutional and Maturational Variations

Luke has motor-planning and sequencing challenges, especially in the gross-motor area. He gets physically overwhelmed and can't rely on his body to regulate and control himself. Instead, he tries to do it mentally and, as a kid, by isolating himself a bit or narrowing the field of engagement so he wouldn't get so overwhelmed. Luke still does that to a degree, but less so now, and we want to help him do this even less and develop other coping capacities so that he will be superior in his ability to cope, and not have to rely on narrowing his field and withdrawing, or resort to dysregulation as his main means of coping. His situation is complicated by the fact that Luke is very sensitive and has a very reactive sensory system.

### Game Plan

It sounds like Luke is a youngster who has gotten everyone to care for him a great deal and admire his many positive abilities as well as a person. It's lovely to hear from his parents and the staff. It sounds like the staff has a basically good program outline for Luke. The key now is to see what additional touches we want to add to keep Dad's goal of expanding his interests and range and flexibility and also help Luke become more of a gray-area thinker and not an all-or-nothing person and move on to reflective thinking and more advanced social skills where he can intuitively sense how to approach a person and how to joke with someone, the things he found hard to do when he was very little.

We want to have lots of building of intimacy and increase in emotional range for Luke. We want to help him identify the feelings he has difficulty with, like loss, anger, and disappointment. Everyone who works with Luke should focus on having long conversations with him, talking for longer and longer periods of time, so he gets used to the rhythm of interpersonal interactions that go over fifteen or twenty minutes. Use the Floortime philosophy of following his interests, talking about robots or music, but let him take the lead and embellish it with trying to explore how he feels, why he feels that way, be appropriately curious about his creative ideas. Also, make this a two-way street and share your ideas and don't be afraid to disagree with him. Get him used to a little conflict or challenge to his ideas. Gradually increase the challenge over the next six months so he gets used to real interpersonal relationships.

When you are talking with him about music, drama, a book or math, in one-on-one Floortime, in the classroom with his educators, try to divide your time doing this with Luke into two parts: One, where you really follow the Floortime philosophy in following his leads and interests, and two, where you have reality-based conversations talking about politics, about the real world, and creating more conflict. If he starts getting agitated or dysregulated, obviously become more soothing and ask him how he's feeling and what you can do together to help him feel more organized because you could see that when you were disagreeing with him he got upset. Ask what the two of you can do. I want Luke to identify the moments before he becomes dysregulated, to be able to identify what it feels like.

Do the "Thinking About Tomorrow" game, or anticipatory problem solving, with Luke three or four times a day. Take a real situation now and project it into the future (tomorrow) where he gets upset or dysregulated and explore how he feels in those situations, how the other person feels, what he routinely does (gets agitated and narrows the field) and what alternatives there are.

At home, parents should do the same thing: half the time follow Luke's lead, half the time have reality-based conversations. Don't shy away from conflict, but when you see him getting upset then switch gears to "How can we help you calm down? What are you feeling?" Have long conversations with Luke where you don't lose him. Also, when he is building things or working on the computer, join him in his activities and interact with him.

We want Luke to be exposed to more situations in which he can apply his creativity. Go out into the world a little more often, going to museums, visiting different areas of the city. The key is to recognize how he feels about going out without a toy. You can do this as part of the "Thinking About Tomorrow" game. Explore why he needs to be "bribed" and how much you are willing to negotiate and make it have some edge to it, like you are the North Koreans. Treat it real and honestly and have fun with it and create a little edgy conflict and try to get the best of him and have him try to get the best of you. Try to get him to do more for his toy and he'll try to get a bigger toy rather than doing more. Set up contests so whoever wins a walking race in the last two blocks, he either gets a more expensive toy or a less expensive one. Set it up so it's an even deal, but let him win seventy percent of the time, initially, and then fifty–fifty, giving yourself a bit of a handicap if necessary. Make it fun and more interactive.

In Luke's Floortime at school and at home, get into some imaginative work, either writing stories about the robots or imaginative play with the robots using his own creations. For at least an hour every day, Luke should be paired with other children who are verbal and bright, both at the Rebecca School as well as at other schools, so he can build friendships and get used to a broader range of children. At home, Luke should have more play dates, particularly on Saturdays and Sundays. The parents may be able to find suitable peers (as young as ten years old) to come to the home from the student population at the Rebecca School or another school.

In terms of Luke's nonverbal behavior, use lots of animation and give him direct feedback. When he's too close, "Oh, I can't talk to you while you're on top of me!" Make your face and voice animated. You can do some psychodramas with pretending to be on top of someone and approaching them gracefully and skillfully. Do this both at school and at home.

Appeal to Luke's visual sense all the time. When he has difficulty grasping a concept, create a visual (like a robot or a sculpture) that conveys the feeling. You can use figures of his own creation, and do imaginative play with his own toys, exploring their feelings.

Take a light touch with Luke, kibitzing and joking with him a lot, and having fun together. Don't take Luke so seriously, like he's a piece of glass that's going to break. It's key to make this a part of your everyday interactions with him so that he gets a sense of an informal, light, kibitzing approach to life. This is what is missing in his life and has made it difficult because if we react in kind to what he does, that will only dig the hole deeper.

Increasing Luke's emotional terrain will make all the difference for him over the next few years. Let's monitor Luke closely because he has great potential and has all the tools.

### Program Responses to Dr. Greenspan's Recommendations

Today, two years later, Luke and one of his teachers ride together toward Luke's home after his after-school soccer program. They ride casually together, talking. The teacher has no fear that he is going to act out, no fear that he will act in a way that will get him in trouble in a New York City subway. They talk quietly across a number of subjects, none of which includes robots. This didn't happen magically. There were months where on their walk they attempted to embarrass each other, months where the teacher actually had to yell inappropriately and roll on the sidewalk, much to Luke's chagrin. There was always the greatest joy and love in the teasing, light-side approach, but he learned that there were things you did and did not do on the streets. He learned that there is a time and a place for different things. He is not perfect at this, but he is beginning to get the idea. For instance, he leaned over to her the other day, and whispered, carefully, so that no one would hear, "Oh my God! Look at that guy on the other side of the car. He is just so fat!" No one else heard, and that is a life-changing difference. Luke has much to do. He still misinterprets signals from his peers, touches people without their permission, speaks to people in situations where his input is not welcome. His adolescent urges and priorities are the same for Luke as other teens, and so he is also dealing with all of he interpersonal challenges of dealing with the opposite sex. However, this is the boy, young man really, who recently came close to kissing a girl in his class. The teacher said, "I stopped you, or you would have kissed her."

"You didn't stop us," Luke said. "We got closer together, and we started laughing. You get anxious and you just start laughing. That's a sure way to mess up romance!"

*Chapter 15*

# To the Other Side of the World and Back . . . For You

I see every child enter the school every day, and it is a real joy to see kids skipping down the street laughing as they come off their buses. They are so happy to be here, and I feel it is a real sign of the health of the school that kids, many of whom were so unhappy going to schools before, run to the door, eager to see their teachers and go to their classrooms. Paul is right in the middle of this group, laughing and pushing his way in as fast as he can. Mom assures me that this was not always the case.

So many of the parents I have spoken to in my work with children with Neurodevelopmental Disorders of Relating and Communicating say that their child had typical births, hit all the developmental milestones within typical limits, and were bright engaged children. Paul's mom is just like this. It wasn't until he was about a year old that she says, "We began to see the signs of what we know now is Autism. He started to flap his hands, he had very loud vocal stimming, and he was holding his breath. I rushed him to the pediatrician's office, and he assured me it was okay. 'Kids do that,' he said." At fifteen months, Paul was exposed to tuberculosis. He tested positive, so Mom had to give him antibiotics for six months. "It was horrific," she now says. "Basically, I had to shove it in his mouth, and hold his mouth closed until he swallowed it. After that, he lost the few words he was saying. His hand flapping went crazy, he stopped answering to his name, and the pediatrician said, 'Maybe he's deaf.' "

Of course, the parents had Paul's hearing tested, and that was within normal ranges, so that was ruled out. They didn't have any idea what was going on. She was told, 'He's a boy. You have to wait.' That's what everybody told me. On his second birthday is when I knew something was really wrong. I remember, I took out the cake, and he refused to blow out the candles. To comfort myself I said, 'Maybe he just needs a nap.' But, he didn't want to nap. He wanted nothing to do with me. He just took a book, sat in a corner, and wanted nothing to do with anybody. That's when he started to cut himself off from everybody. This was a kid who used to answer the phone, who answered the door, who ran to the door when his Dad came home from work screaming, 'Daddy, Daddy, Daddy!' Then, I don't know. He was not my kid anymore. I always explain it, that someone came and stole my kid's insides, and left me with a shell. I no longer knew him."

Like many moms and dads, Paul's mom really got a clearer idea of the degree of the problem when she enrolled her son in play groups and kids' programs. At two years old she had the chance to compare him to typically developing kids, and she was surprised at the level of Paul's deficits. The contacts she made there got her to take Paul to a developmental pediatrician, and he got the diagnosis of PDD-NOS. He was soon enrolled in intervention, and he received ABA, speech and OT. "Paul hated ABA, but I let it go for eight months, because I wanted to give it a chance to work. It didn't work, so I stopped it. During the ABA, he got very, very aggressive. He loved the speech and OT, because the therapists were nice to him. I wouldn't say he made much progress, but it wasn't so bad.

"He went to another school after that, where he was in a 12–1–1 class, and he got totally lost. He got ABA there, and speech and OT again. He hated it. It was horrible to drag him to school every morning where he hated it. He stopped saying anything; he was not saying any words, not even, 'No' or 'Yes.' I would drag him to the bus, I would put him on, and it was a nightmare. Seeing him like that . . . I had to pull him out. I took him to my parents."

Mom's parents live in Malta. This mother felt that she could not get services here, and took her son to her home country, in hopes of finding someone who could understand her son, where he would make progress, not regress. "In Malta, he was placed in a regular classroom with a shadow. He also received therapy outside school. When I saw the large class, and I looked at what was happening, I knew in my heart that he wasn't going to make any progress. So, once again, we came back to New York. Now, he was five. We enrolled in a public school special-ed classroom. I liked the program because there was no ABA, so I knew that he was not going to get so angry and aggressive. He did well. I was in the school much of the time, to help the teacher and Paul connect, but we saw progress. He took the first few steps to independence. He tied his shoes; he got dressed. He got potty trained immediately. His first year there he loved his teacher, and he did well. The second year he loved his new teacher, she was sweet, so he made progress.

"I went to a medical doctor at this time, because I wanted to try chelation. This doctor talked me out of it, and suggested I try vitamins first. He wanted to get his body ready in case we decided to try chelation. He had B-12 injections, iron, calcium, and a multivitamin. He also started probiotics, enzymes, omega-3; he takes six different kinds, twice a day. I have to measure it for him. On these vitamins, his speech peaked. He went from saying 'weird' words, he would say 'at' for 'cat,' 'cookie' was '*ooo ahh*' for example. His father and I were the only ones who knew what he was saying. When he went to school and asked for something, he was not understood. By February, though, his speech got clearer, and he could say, 'cat' and 'doggie.'

"In the summer, he moved to the next site of the school, and he did not like this as he did not know anyone at this school. Soon after this, my father died, and I had to go home for three days, and it was hard on me, and I think it was hard on him. When I got home, I had to rush him to the hospital with appendicitis. Soon after, my biomedical doctor suggested we try hyperbaric treatment. I looked into it, and I did not see any harm in it, so we rented a chamber. Paul loved it! He would come home from school, and jump into it all on his own. In the first month, he did fifty-four hours of hyperbaric treatment, where he had to sit there for an hour-and-a-half at a time. He did it beautifully!"

"In May, he was hurt in school. He came home with markings on his legs. I think that's when everything went haywire. Paul got very aggressive. His behavior changed. I rented the chamber again, and it was a nightmare. From him jumping in it happily, he was screaming and crying. He did not want to go in it. I had no idea what to do. I did force him to go in it. We did get one-hundred-and-twenty-nine hours. I don't know what good it did, because we did not see any progress. None whatsoever. I never rented another chamber again.

"Paul started this year at the Rebecca School, and what a change! I never have to drag him out of my house, drag him down the stairs to bring him to school. He happily wakes up in the morning, does all of his morning routines, goes into his bedroom to change, and comes downstairs. It's unbelievable to see such a change in such a short amount of time. Paul's speech has also really come along. Out of the blue he is saying to me, 'Mom, I want milk and cookies, please,' 'I want water, please.' It's an amazing change. And he is saying the words more clearly now. One day we were standing at the bus stop and I asked him, 'What's the weather like?' and I was going to continue, and he interrupted and said, 'It's raining.' And I was totally shocked! So the next day I asked him, sometimes I don't believe what I hear him say—" Mom got choked up. She continued, "I asked him, 'What's the weather like?' and he said, 'It's sunny.' So I knew he was with it, and that these answers had not been drilled into him! And that's what I want. I don't want him to be robotic, I want him to tell me what he sees, what he feels."

Paul's program at Rebecca School includes his time in one of the most active classes in the school with six other boys all around his age. Some of the boys have more language than he does, but some do not, and none are any more physically able than him. He has certain skills that he brings to the class, that his classmates appreciate, and although he was a new addition to a class of boys who had already known each other, in some cases, for years, he fit right in. He has five or six Floortime sessions a day in the classroom, and other physical activities aimed at his visual-spatial processing and motor planning. In addition, he gets individual speech therapy and occupational therapy, as well as art and music therapy. He is very attentive, and the class spends much of its time with him helping him to stay receptive and ready for interaction, and helping to support his attempts at interaction and problem solving. He gets very upset over changes in routine.

A teaching assistant in the class, John, talks about his best interaction in a case conference in front of the entire school. "I came over with a couple of puppets, and I had them on my hand and he pointed to the puppets and said, 'Off.' I thought, *'Oh no, he doesn't like puppets.'* The staff laughed as John told the story. "But then, he pointed to one puppet and said, 'Fox.' I said, 'Sure.' I gave him the fox and he put it on his hand. Then he pointed to the panda bear and said, 'Panda.' And he started to smash them against his chest really hard. So I put on a monkey, and said, 'Monkey,' at this point John put on a high, squeaky, monkey voice, "and I said, 'Mister Monkey squish too.'" The staff is laughing hysterically at this point. "And he points to himself and says, 'Sqoosh.' So I gave him a sqoosh and he really liked that. 'Oh,'" (again in the monkey voice) "'Can Mister Monkey get a sqoosh?' He lunges at me and squeezes me really hard. Normally he is a really reserved kid, but when he sqooshes you he puts every ounce of his being into it!" The staff continues to laugh as John gets more and more enthusiastic in his recitation of the interaction. "So we squish back and forth for a bit, and then he sort of swats at his monkey with his panda, so I said, (in the monkey voice) 'Oh, you and Mister Monkey kiss?' And there was no response. Then he swats at it again and I say (monkey voice) 'Ouch, ouch don't hit me!' And he cracks up, he really likes it! When he is dysregulated he is big on hitting us pretty hard. He started whacking the monkey, and I was saying, (monkey) 'Oh no you can't get me! I'm hiding on the beanbag chair!' And he jumps on the beanbag chair, and he chased me around for a while. He did some pretty complex things, like he would track the puppet while I would move him around, he would pick up boxes and search for places where the puppet would hide; he would really do a lot to swat this monkey! So now, he is seeking me out and initiating this game with me, he'll grab a penguin and want to smack a puppet I have."

When they played together as part of their initial interview with me for admission, there was almost no talking between Paul and Mom. When I coughed, it seemed almost startlingly loud, so silent was their play at the dollhouse. Mom handed him dollhouse furniture, which he dutifully placed into the house. He fooled with a truck as she searched the bin for a particular piece of furniture; he placed a baby in a crib on the roof, and then moved to the next task. Neither of them was having a particularly good time. The strength of their bond was apparent, her intense caring, and his equally intense desire to comply and please her was there. But there was an assembly-line quality to the proceedings. There was no joy.

Mom asked to become part of the Parent Training Course I ran at that time with the gifted Floortime Specialist at our school, Alex. She showed us videos of herself working with Paul at home. I saw a repeat of the admissions doll house assembly, but this time, Paul was angry. Mom was well versed in techniques that used a lot of prompting, and compliance. He resisted terribly. He would look away from the task, refuse to vocalize, passively resist, and if she insisted he would begin to get agitated and remove the objects she wanted him to identify from the table. He got angrier and angrier, making a vocalization that indicated his anger, and eventually he just turned away and left the situation, while Mom asked him to come back to the table. She sat there for a moment, and the video ended with her getting up and shutting off the camera.

With a lot of feedback Mom came back week after week with video, always with Mom's frustration at his lack of language showing. As the culmination of the course, we would do a live coaching session with the mother and the child. Alex coached them as I taped. We went to the sensory gym, and let Paul and Mom play. She took the suggestion to use the swing as a way to get him going back and forth with him in a flow, she would push, then stop, while he excitedly giggled and wanted her to push again. Alex told her to use this opportunity to get him to let her know what he wanted. He gestured for her to push. She did. Then she stopped, and he asked again. She pushed. Then he fell off, so they added a crash into the game, and before too long, across a number of different situations they had a laughing, pushing, giggling back and forth for a half an hour. The session ended, and Paul went back to class. Mom had a gleam in her eye, but she was also fighting back tears. "I have never had such a back and forth with my son in my life! That is the most we have communicated, ever. I get it. You need to find what he likes, and that is the way in!"

Everything about Mom's actions in the time since that breakthrough session indicates that she does, indeed, get it. She has wholeheartedly embraced the model, and works, or more properly, plays with him at home in a way she never did before. She even talked about the changes in Paul's art. Before he came to Rebecca School, he had always liked art, and Mom made sure that he had plenty of materials. However, all he would ever do was, take his crayons, or his watercolors, and paint lines on a piece of paper, systematically, in the order in which he took them from the box. "I had thousands of these line paintings," Mom says. She holds her hands up to indicate a pile about four feet high. "He seemed to like doing it, so I always made sure he had crayons and paper, but I hoped he would do something different." Since he has had art therapy at the school, however, his art has changed. He varies his techniques, works with different media, is willing to smear and blend, and generally has abandoned the rigid lines of the past. As a final acknowledgment of Paul's change and hard work, some of his art recently won an award at a regional art show!

### Sensory and Motor Strengths and Challenges as Understood and Described by the Rebecca School Staff

*Visual Spatial:*

- Easily distracted visually.
- Pays particular attention to rapid movement in his visual field.

- Will move his hand in the periphery of his visual field. While it can be distracting for him, visual-spatial processing is a relative strength.
- Adept at reading gestures such as points, shrugs, and facial cues.

### Auditory:

- Easily overstimulated.
- Although this is not always an indication of auditory sensitivity, will cover his ears in response to loud or chaotic noise.
- Processing is a difficulty for him.

### Proprioceptive:

- Finds proprioceptive feedback regulating, and will seek it out. Came to Rebecca School already stamping his feet violently when trying to get himself under control; now will crash into a beanbag chair, wear a weighted vest, use a weighted blanket, or seek out deep pressure from a staff person.

### Vestibular:

- Seeks input by hanging off his chair so his head is in an inverted position or by quickly moving about the room with no apparent purpose but to move.

### Tactile:

- Has no apparent tactile defensiveness.

### Motor Processing and Planning:

- This is a real area of strength. When regulated he can motor plan with ease through a seven- or eight-step obstacle course.
- Has good bilateral coordination and good fine-motor skills. He can write his name independently. Appears to find fine-motor activities regulating.

## Rebecca School Program in Place Before Consulting with Dr. Greenspan

*Floortime: 4–6 x 20 min./day, Individual, in the classroom, with teacher or one specific teaching assistant, primarily.*

- Focus on Level I, to help Paul stay regulated, and Level II, emerging Level III. With support in the classroom, Paul can go back and forth for eight to ten circles of communication.

*Speech: 4 x 30 min./week, Individual.*

- Oral-motor therapy, articulation therapy, PROMPT, and language intervention, emphasis on the DIR Model. Paul is capable of interaction in a continuous flow for fifteen to thirty minutes in the supportive and quiet environment of a one-on-one speech session.

*OT: 3 x 30 min./week, Indvidual.*

- Proprioceptive and vestibular work in support of Levels I, II, and III. Therapist can get thirty circles of communication in a continuous flow in a one-on-one situation with Paul when he is engaged in gross-motor activities. She has seen difficulty with his initiation in problem solving, and no fantasy play.

*Music Therapy: 1 x 30 min./week.*

*Art Therapy: 2 x 20 min./week, with two peers.*

- Has shown Level IV and emerging Level IV thinking in his willingness to abandon previously rigid use of materials, with problem solving and experimentation to express clear ideas he has for his art.

## Dr. Greenspan's Recommendations

Paul is ten-and-a-third years old, and is doing very well at the Rebecca School. He has a history of being diagnosed with PDD and ASD. Paul had ABA therapy early in his development, but got very aggressive and dysregulated with it and didn't like it. Paul can stay calm and regulated, but when he gets dysregulated he is sensory seeking, active, and aggressive. This can happen off and on. Paul's real strength is in his engagement, but he has a hard time initiating the engagement. He can be purposeful and a two-way communicator, with an average of eight to ten circles and up to forty to fifty when motivated. We want to get into a continuous flow so he does it all the time with everyone.

Paul can sequence and problem solve. He can use words and gestures to problem solve. He has solid abilities, but needs to do it more. He can use ideas. He can understand simple directions and do multiple choice now, so Paul is moving into the world of ideas more and more. The intriguing part is the inconsistency and unevenness of it, of his use of ideas. On the one hand, you see fairly complex complete sentences, following directions and doing some complex thinking, and yet at other times he's having trouble with the basic "W" questions. He is beginning to combine some ideas together with multiple choice and sometimes answering some "W" questions; however, he is not yet answering "Why" questions. He is showing some islands of combining ideas together.

### Constitutional and Maturational Variations

Paul biggest challenge is in auditory-processing and language, with the expressive being harder for him than the receptive. Fine and gross motor are a relative strength for him. He is very overreactive to visual input and he can become sensory seeking. He shows mixed reactivity. His visual-spatial processing is a relative strength for Paul and we want to strengthen it further.

### Game Plan

Here are a few suggestions to enhance what's already a very nice program for Paul. He likes everyone and others seem to like him as well, even though he can get dysregulated and irritate people at times. Because Paul has some unevenness in his ability where he shows higher level abilities than he is able to do all the time, we have to assume that there is a strong emotional piece involved here. So, we want to assign one or two of the staff to be his primary person(s) so he can learn to really trust someone. The example with the puppet play is a good one, and maybe that person could be a primary to try and work with Paul. This person should always be available for Paul and maybe we will see more of the higher levels functioning more of the time as he begins to trust this person and build the relationship. The one-on-one person should be doing at least six twenty minute Floortime sessions a day with Paul working on all these things. Everyone else can augment that with the other parts of his program.

Because Paul does things when he is highly motivated, we have to work off his passions a little more. Create opportunities in the classroom where he can do the kinds of sensory things he likes so that he's highly motivated most of the time. This is when he takes the initiative and we will get more things cooking that way.

Paul's strong in the visual-spatial and motor areas, so we definitely want to use pictures all around so he can show you what he wants, but have him say the word too. This should be done at home as well. Provide lots of visual support. Paul is the kind of child who, because he has good motor skills, may be able to learn to type and read and that could augment his verbal abilities. Have the words under the pictures and use that to prompt the verbal and also see if he shows any interest in learning to use a computer or other typing system or write. We should encourage him to use reading and writing in communication, not just as separate academic exercises. Give him the option of writing what he wants. Read the word under the picture and tell us what he wants. Use his strengths a little bit more.

Paul's the kind of child who works best off of action because his motor system is strong. We don't want to focus on conversation alone, but conversation with action. Always be doing something along with the conversation. Be involved in physical action where the dialogue builds on the action. Then bring in pictures or words to help him express what he wants to say. We want to give him multiple routes for communication, but it should be off of action. He should be having two twenty-minute sessions doing the *Thinking Goes to School* exercises. See how high he can go. Keep his visual-spatial thinking cooking.

At home, parents should try to do four Floortime sessions in the evening—mother, two sessions and father two sessions—where you harness his initiative and work off interactions he likes. Consult with the school weekly (staff can coach parents on ways to bring Paul out) to identify activities he likes that can be created at home as well. Lots more verbal and action exchanges. He should have no more than forty-five minutes a day of alone time. Most of the time someone should be interacting with him.

These additions to the already good program should help Paul make faster progress.

### Rebecca School's Response to Dr. Greenspan's Recommendations

In the classroom, one primary TA, the one with the "example with the puppet play" became Paul's primary "go-to" person. This TA, John, has also gone to get extensive training in the *Thinking Goes to School* exercises, and with the support of the rest of the staff and school has made this into a curriculum for the class. One of the primary beneficiaries has been Paul, and he has made visual-spatial and motor progress. These *Thinking Goes to School* sessions are always conducted with an emphasis on DIR Levels and goals, and so, an effort is made to support Paul in a continuous flow while he is crossing his midline, for instance.

In speech, Paul has begun with a picture communication book, which he uses in support of his spoken language. Plans are under way for him to use an augmentative communication device, and tailoring one that meets his needs and supports his emerging language are prime considerations.

With a dedicated family, devoted staff, bouncing peers, and an indomitable spirit, Paul, like all the kids at Rebecca School, will continue to work in relationships, according to their own individual differences, to grow, grow, grow!

## Chapter 16

# Popcorn

I look at the video of my intake with Raymond two-and-a-half years ago, and I marvel at the little boy sitting in front of me. I look much the same, but he has changed entirely on the outside. Then, he was a little, smooth-skinned youth, and now he is an adolescent, much bigger, on his way to being a young man. Then, he seemed so small and passive, and now, he has become a force to be reckoned with, the focus of much attention at Rebecca School. I watch and listen to the video, and slowly the Raymond I have come to know and appreciate unfolds in front of me. He fiddles absently with a toy I have laid out on the floor, hunched over, with his legs crossed, and asks me questions. I answer them dutifully, and slowly it dawns on the taped me that he already knows the answer to much of what he asks. That hasn't changed. The young Raymond talks about things he has memorized, things that are related to calendars and time, and I recognize this too, from the Raymond of today. I see the earlier me get a little urgent about wanting to entice him into an interaction, and the younger Raymond resists this. He will not be enticed into the world of abstraction and interaction until a highly skilled clinician comes along later in his Rebecca School career, one who is willing to, and understands why it is important to, take her time with him.

Raymond spent his first two years at Rebecca School in a classroom with seven other boys, with the most diverse developmental profiles. In the class there was a boy who had lost his hearing at eighteen months, and so lost his language, a boy with Fragile X syndrome, several boys whose disabilities fell somewhere on the neurodevelopmental spectrum, and a boy who spent the first seven years of his life in a Romanian orphanage. It is difficult to imagine a more diverse group, yet Raymond fit in, and was never a particular problem. But he never particularly thrived or made any documentable progress up the FEDMs either. He moved parallel to the other kids, negotiating the world by virtue of his great memory, asking disarming questions, and freaking out at the end of the day, almost every day by the end of year two. The fact that Raymond's lack of movement was not really noted is a tribute to how well he gets along by using his prodigious memory and careful attention.

I have never before known a kid who could keep accurate time in his head. Raymond can, over the course of the entire day, to the minute, even while in the middle of the most active, chaotic situation. I remember the old *Let's Make a Deal* with Monty Hall, where Monty would offer a hundred dollars to an audience member if she could tell him when twenty-five seconds had elapsed while he kept her busy talking. The audience member could almost never do it, and neither could I watching at home. Yet, Raymond seemed to be able to do it over the course of a long and action-packed day. I first realized this when a Floortime therapist was running a "Russian social club" with Raymond and Oleg. Alla came to me later and told me that Raymond had said to her, at the end of a very active session in the Floortime room, "Alla, it's ten-twenty-nine. Is it time to go back to the classroom?" Alla looked around, saw that there was no clock or watch in the room, pulled her phone out of her purse, and looked at the time. Ten twenty-nine. Later, she said to me, "There was no way he could have known, except that he kept the time in his head!" I had trouble believing it, so I went into the room and looked around. No DVR blinked the time, no tower on 30th Street out the window had a clock, there was no way he could have seen the time. I went and asked Melanie, his classroom teacher of two years, if it could be true. "Oh yeah, he keeps the time in his head. He always has, as long as I've known him." She said it matter-of-factly, as if this were something that all kids did ordinarily.

He also memorizes things. He has the sort of transit fetish that many New York City kids at our school have, and can tell you how to get almost anywhere in the five boroughs without consulting a map. He will ask where you live, and then will figure out in his head how to get from his house to yours. Google Earth has been a boon to him, and after asking you where you live you may walk into the computer lab to see the roof of your house, or the top of your apartment building staring back at you from Raymond's monitor. He knows unwritten lines of demarcation between neighborhoods as well as the lifelong natives of those neighborhoods; for example, he recently told a staff member that she did not live in Park Slope proper, but in South Park Slope.

When he walks into a room he looks at the walls, and if there are schedules posted he studies them intensely. It takes him almost no time to commit them to memory, and he has good recall of them later on. My office has an entire wall with all of the schedules of all the classrooms and all the therapists in the school. This, to Raymond is a kind of heaven. It isn't that he is being nosey, he just needs to have all the factual information about all the staff and students that is available, so that he can converse on those topics later with everyone he encounters. Furthermore, this is Raymond's coping strategy, a way of piecing together the world surrounding him. In addition to the growing number of students and teachers at Rebecca, semesters of student teachers from nearby universities, psychology interns and externs, as well as the rest of our young staff, where someone is always either leaving for graduate school or moving to another country to find themselves, there is a lot of information to keep track of. For Raymond, being as social and inquisitive as he is, but not yet a solid abstract thinker, it is not enough to just hear, "Oh, she is going back to school." He isn't able to create a mental image or scenario that makes sense, putting things in perspective, and he has trouble explaining why a certain person has ceased to exist in his concrete world.

Raymond's anxious, question-asking helped him through the first year at Rebecca, and served him through at least the beginning of the second year. However, as the second year wore on, Raymond got more and more agitated. The end of the day was the bane of his existence. He would get extremely upset whenever the end of the day rolled around, and when his classroom teacher wrote in his communication book. "No! You wrote a note! Don't!" Raymond would scream and cry, and move back and forth as agitated as he could possibly be. His classroom teachers would try to reassure him that the note said nothing bad. It could be that he had misinterpreted a word in the note, or he may have actually destroyed something during the day, or tried to pull someone's hair, or scratched someone. The actual facts did not appear to matter to Raymond. He looked fearful, and cried that he was afraid that something bad would happen to him at home. The drama would leave the classroom, and a group of teachers would travel through the school with Raymond, as he moved toward the front door.

In the main vestibule of the school the drama would continue. Raymond would scream and cry, his teachers would surround him with assurance that everything would be alright, that the note was innocuous, and that he should get on the bus. He would not. The bus drivers and matrons would get annoyed, as they had other kids on the bus they needed to deliver, staff would get frazzled, and Raymond would continue to be distraught, until he would reluctantly get on the bus. This same scene, played out in remarkably similar ways, marked the end of virtually every day of Raymond's second year.

At the beginning of Raymond's third year, we moved him into a classroom with kids who were his same chronological age, with all different developmental levels. Around this time, Raymond, now fourteen, began to get aggressive with his peers and with the adults in the class. He began to pinch and scratch people, in a way unlike his previous behavior. He began to pull women's hair, and really hurt them. Kids in the class began to fear him, and the staff felt that they had to spend much of their time separating him from his peers. They saw him as a major problem, someone whose behavior required strict attention, and so he became the focus of the class. Soon, the staff began to fear him too. The women all began to wear their hair up, and tried to stay away from him. They flinched if he walked past. If they found themselves in the elevator with him and another therapist, they would get off so that they would not get hurt. He became the number one subject of meetings around the school, the subject of much of the talk in the staff lounge. Soon, parents of other students in the class began to protest how dangerous he was to their children, and eventually the crisis level was reached. A decision was made, and Raymond was removed from the class to follow an individual schedule.

As one of the directors of the school, admittedly, I can get somewhat isolated from particular kids and their circumstances, and so I did not really know what was going on in Raymond's life outside of school. I had the vague sense that the parents were not around the school in the way that other parents often were. I began to see that people were feeling protective about Raymond and their communications home, as typified by the way they handled him so gingerly at the end of each school day. I did not understand why, exactly. So, I began to ask questions. At team meetings it became clear that Raymond had convinced the team of some great menace he faced at home, never clearly stated, and that they now acted as if this were a reality. I followed up with his social worker, new to his case this year, and she stated that the parents were always responsive to her, but that she just got the sense that there was some kind of reason why it was necessary to be careful what you said to them, although she couldn't really put her finger on it. Meanwhile, Raymond deteriorated. He was out of his classroom, with a one-on-one all day, receiving services, but missing out on the rich classroom and peer experience he deserved.

We decided to bring the case to Dr. Greenspan for his suggestions. This is a pretty big event, and so parents generally jump at the chance. When the day came for their conference with Dr. Greenspan, the parents did not come. Their absence thickened the fog around the family dynamics. American parents jump at the chance to speak with Dr. Greenspan, Alla points out, because they have done their research on interventions available, and because, there is not the stigma associated with special needs that there is in Russia. In addition, parent-teacher conferences were held the following night and Mom could not leave work early two days in a row. I did not really understand this until I met them two days later, so I labored under this series of cultural biases for a little longer. Raymond's social worker tried to represent them, but she had scant information. She had no developmental history, no current medication list, or any information about any treatment he may have been getting outside of Rebecca School. "I am Raymond's social worker, and I'm just going to read you the social history, and tomorrow his mother is going to come, and so at least we will be able to give her all your recommendations."

"Don't read it to me. Just give me the highlights of the social history," Dr. Greenspan said.

"Okay." She started hesitantly, laying out the particulars of the family. It was clear that she had very little information, and it even seemed to me that the reporter for some of the information was Raymond himself. She said, "His older sister is nineteen, and she is in college for pre-med, and she shares a room with Raymond." She went on to outline what she knew, in a very abbreviated form what she had been able to piece together from her various sources. She began to speak about his classroom history at Rebecca School. "He was placed in a classroom with seven other boys. He had a hard time understanding why he was not placed in an older classroom, because he was a little bit older than the other kids in the classroom. He was really aware of the difference."

Only toward the end did I hear his family's voice. Briefly, the social worker read the summary of what Mom had said about her son. "Mom described Raymond as a very enthusiastic, inquisitive, and sweet boy. He likes to go to various outings and play, however, doesn't enjoy things that require a lot of time and concentration as he easily gets bored. He is easily distracted and she finds he has a hard time refocusing and he can become very hyper. She feels that though he enjoys all these activities and is very curious, he has a difficult time interacting with his peers." I felt as if a window had been cracked open, for the briefest of moments, and I saw a ray of light illuminating how the family actually saw their son and brother. They loved him, they cherished him, and it gave me the confidence to renew our efforts to help this family with their boy.

### Sensory and Motor Strengths and Challenges as Understood and Described by the Rebecca School Staff

*Visual Spatial:*

- Good visual acuity.
- Has a tremendous spatial understanding of his world.
- Has difficulty generating an original motor plan based on his visual perception.

*Auditory:*

- Good auditory acuity.
- Difficulty filtering ambient noise in the environment.
- Auditory processing delay.

*Proprioceptive:*

- Jumps, flaps, and claps.
- Seeks intense proprioceptive input, and is calmer after this.
- Input helps him to motor plan.

*Vestibular:*

- Seeks all sorts of vestibular input, in all planes.
- Becomes dizzy with very little rotational input.

*Tactile:*

- Displays no tactile sensitivities.

*Motor Processing and Planning:*

- Difficulty with gross-motor skills.
- Low overall tone.
- Weak core, inhibiting planning and execution.

## Rebecca School Program in Place Before Consulting
## with Dr. Greenspan

*Floortime: 4–6 x 20 min./day, Individual, in the classroom, and in the larger ecological setting.*

*Speech: 3 x 30 min./week, Individual.*

- Oral-motor protocol, in session and in classroom.

*OT: 2 x 30 min./week, Individual, 1 x 30 min./week, in a movement group with five to seven others.*

*Counseling: 1 x 30 min./week, Individual.*

*Music Therapy: 1 x 30 min./week.*

*Art Therapy: 2 x 20 min./week, with two peers.*

## Dr. Greenspan's Recommendations

Raymond is an adolescent boy who is fourteen-years-old. As we hear about him, we note that he has a history of a diagnosis of ASD and has attended a number of different schools before Rebecca School. In terms of the different Milestones Raymond has achieved and his current level of functioning, Raymond can focus, attend, engage, interact, do social problem solving, use ideas and language creatively and meaningfully, and can connect ideas together and answer all the "W" questions, including "Why" questions. Raymond can also do multi-causal thinking, but is not yet at the level of doing gray-area or reflective thinking. At all these developmental levels, Raymond is very restricted in his range and how elaborative and creative he can get. Raymond can get dysregulated easily and then gets impulsive and physical.

## Constitutional and Maturational Variations

Raymond has auditory-processing and language challenges with receptive language challenges. He could use some help in motor planning and sequencing, and needs to have a better sense of his body in space. He tends to overreact and become dysregulated, impulsive, and inappropriately physical. He has visual-spatial processing challenges and tends to get caught up in the details rather than seeing the big picture.

## Game Plan

Everyone is working very well with Raymond, but I think that Raymond experiences a lot of overload and fragmentation. Each one of the teachers/therapists is doing very well with him individually, but collectively there are too many chefs stirring the pot. Thus, Raymond is having different experiences with so many different people trying to help him become a better thinker that I think he is repeating the same things over and over again. He is clearly preoccupied with issues regarding adolescence, issues having to do with the body, desires, and urges. He doesn't know what to do with these urges and desires and asks lots of questions because his expressive language is stronger than his receptive. So, how do we prepare an adolescent like Raymond for adulthood? The following suggestions will help strengthen and unify Raymond's program at the Rebecca School.

Raymond should have at least six Floortime sessions each day with just a couple of people being the main ones to work with him during these sessions. Also, Raymond should have a male therapist who can become a mentor for him. Focus a little more on the feeling side of things with Raymond, helping him become a poet of his feelings and get into gray-area thinking about feelings. When he's asking questions about a teacher or therapist, he is really trying to orient himself in space. He should have a very strong visual-spatial program involving the exercises from *Thinking Goes to School*, three to four times each day.

Raymond should have a program that helps him with developing life skills. Assess where his talents are and begin a very active training/academic program that develops and strengthens these talents. He should have an occupational therapy program focusing on body awareness and how to regulate himself better. He may also need an outside therapist (preferably male) who can be with him for the long term. The nurturing and growth that will occur through a one-on-one therapist will be very critical.

In summary, we want to help Raymond get into gray-area thinking, articulate his feelings a bit better, have two primary therapists (male) to help him with the feeling side of life, and develop a strong academic program to help him acquire the life skills he will need when he's eighteen. For any young teenager, we need these kinds of goals.

### Program Responses to Dr. Greenspan's Recommendations

In a conference with Alla about the case, we decided upon an action plan. I would meet with the mother when she came in the following night to meet with the social worker, and offer the family my help, suggesting that we pick a night when they all could come in to talk. Alla would come as the interpreter if needed, and we would see if we could be useful to them. At the very least, we could open a dialogue that would help illuminate why this air of mystery and menace had grown up around our relationship with them.

The next day, around five o'clock, Raymond's mother and sister came in to meet with the social worker. I came into her office, and introduced myself to them. Raymond's mother was kind and quiet, and apologized to me for her bad English. In truth, her English was accented but very good, and we had no trouble talking at all. Raymond's sister was also there, and her English was perfect; she moved fluidly between the two languages. Among us we worked out a plan where the family would come in the following week to talk about Raymond. I asked if Mom thought that Dad would be able to attend, as he seemed to be the one missing in all the conversations I had ever had about Raymond. She and her daughter assured me that Dad would be happy to come. I looked to see if the social worker was as surprised as I was, and she seemed to be, because we had come to believe that it would be very difficult to get the family together for a meeting. We agreed we would all get together the following Monday night.

That week, I spoke to Dr. Greenspan during our supervision time. He asked me what plan I had for kids like Raymond as they began to age out of our program, and took me to task about the older kids. It was then that the words "vocational training" came up, and I lost the ability to be rational. I told Dr. Greenspan of my experiences in group-home work here in New York, and despite having worked at one of the loveliest group settings imaginable, I did not always have good experiences when the clients left our home. I thought of all the ABA programs I had visited with their mock mail rooms and kids delivering paper towels to classrooms with "supply carts." I knew that there was tremendous variability within the vocational training world for kids on the neurodevelopmental spectrum, but I also knew that I wanted nothing to do with most of that world for the kids at Rebecca School. At first it seemed antithetical to the notion of DIR/Floortime to be closing off options for kids. I told Dr. Greenspan so. He said, "Let's take a look at what is keeping you from being able to feel like you can participate in this." This was his way of telling me that somehow I had a transference problem! We talked for a while about what the notion of vocational training meant to me in my experience. Finally he said, "Well Gil, what if we change it from 'vocational training' to 'taking DIR to the larger ecological context'? You wouldn't have an objection to that, would you?" So over the course of the next half hour we talked about taking the Floortime sessions into the community, to cover vocational goals in a Floortime way.

I spoke to Alla later that day about this notion, this "taking DIR to the larger ecological context," and she immediately embraced it, taking it from my theoretical understanding to her applied understanding with the greatest fluidity and grace. Within a day, she had put together a beginning program for Raymond. It involved taking him out into the streets of Manhattan around our school. Remember, by this time, Raymond was no longer in the classroom because his teachers, the students in the class and their parents had come to view him as a danger. He regularly scratched, hit, and pulled the hair of the people around him, particularly the women. It took real expertise to pull off being a smaller woman taking the large and seemingly aggressive teen into the streets of Manhattan, and a keen sense of one's own strengths. I was worried that Alla may be putting herself at risk. She brushed me off. "Oh, don't worry." And she was right.

The next day, Alla set Raymond to work. They called another psychologist in the building who was running a sibling group and asked her what she needed for the group. They got a shopping list from her, and Alla told Raymond that he would earn a quarter for every item they would have to buy. He could decide what he wanted to buy or save for, and they would continue to do this until he bought what he wanted, then they could start saving again. Out the door they went. They stood on the sidewalk. Alla asked him where he thought they should go. He told her where. She stood there. He stood there. She waited for him to give some indication of a plan or an idea. Finally, realizing that she was not going to cue or prompt, he said, "This way," and off they went. They got to the corner and stopped. The crossing sign changed from the red hand to the little white man; they did not move. Raymond seemed to be focusing on something up high, squinting. The hand and little man appeared again in sequence. Alla and Raymond continued to stand there. People, formerly standing still around them started moving across the street. Raymond and Alla stood still. Again the light changed and so did the crossing signal. Raymond was preoccupied with something, so it appeared that none of this was registering. Again and again the light changed, again and again people stepped off the curb around them to cross Park Avenue, but Alla and Raymond stood still. Finally, Raymond roused himself, looked around, and asked, "Alla, shouldn't we cross the street?"

"Is it safe, Raymond?"

He puzzled, looked at the people crossing, and said, "Yes. We should cross now." And so they did.

This scenario, Alla waiting for Raymond to take some action, to process what was going on around him, was repeated thousands of times. In the grocery store, Raymond was attracted to the bright and compelling packaging to read. He would stand in an aisle and scan shelves, not really comprehending that he may have been aisles away from where the snacks he was buying for the sibling group were. Alla would support him, offer him choices if he was really stuck, but basically allowed the slow process to unfold before her. She did not worry if the chips made it to the sibling group, or later, if the supplies from the office store made it to the office manager. She stood still, and created a space for the work to take place. That work was the processing, the thinking that Raymond was doing, no matter how excruciatingly slow it may have been. It is the greatest gift we give kids, the time to think, and Alla gave it to this young man who we could no longer manage in a classroom, and of whom people were afraid.

The following Monday night was set as the appointment for Raymond's family, Alla, and me. I admit I had fears, as there was real trepidation among staff about this family, and Raymond's role in it. As the time approached I got anxious. Then, Raymond's family appeared at the door, smiling, clearly nervous, but apparently happy to be there. We all got in the elevator together, and made our way to my conference room on the sixth floor. When we sat down and got comfortable, after we did introductions, the family began to talk. First, Raymond's older sister began to outline how they experienced him at home. While she spoke of her close relationship with Raymond, of their intimate talks together and her clear adoration of him, the parents beamed. Then Mom talked about her hopes and dreams for him, and again, her love and admiration for his great talents came through. Finally, it was Dad's turn. He had been the one least available to the school by everyone's report, and so he was the one onto whom the most fears and confusion had been projected.

He spoke of his son in the endearing way men speak of their sons as they hit puberty and begin to move from the world of children to the world of men. He clearly admired his son's abilities, and feared for his son in some of his challenges. He talked about rough housing, wrestling and chasing him, laughing with him. And he talked about walking arm in arm with him through his primarily Russian neighborhood, taking in the sights and commenting on the day, proud in the way that other fathers were proud of their sons as they strolled. Here was a man who loved his son, who honored his strengths and challenges, and who wanted the best. He came to us ready for our support and advice. Despite anything we all may have feared and imagined, here was a family ready for our support.

During the meeting, Alla spoke of her relationship with Raymond, the family spoke about their goals and dreams for Raymond, and I helped them understand the DIR model and Floortime a little better. It was clear that everyone was on the same page by the end of the meeting. Here was a young man of great ability, with challenges that we all wanted to understand and help him with. This dedicated family never hesitated; they were ready to do what they had to, to help their beloved son and brother to realize some of his great potential.

The staff, however, was not as easy to convince. They had been physically hurt at times, and they had seen Raymond at his most dysregulated. The head teacher got a lot of pressure from parents who were angry and did not see that Raymond could be a really valuable member of the class. So, when the social worker and I appeared at their team meeting the following Tuesday, with a plan to begin returning Raymond to the class for even the most controlled and circumscribed times, they freaked out. You could see them physically react, and they could not imagine that Raymond could reenter their classroom so soon, or perhaps ever. About five minutes into the meeting I realized that in my zeal to share my enthusiasm over Raymond's loving family and Alla's good work, I had not taken into account how much these people felt they suffered. Every member of the team, from the classroom staff to the therapists had their hair pulled, or were hit, or scratched, and worse, they had seen their classroom kids have the same things done to them. Clearly they were not ready to have Raymond rejoin the classroom.

So, Raymond continued on his out of classroom schedule. I continued seeing the family for my once-a-month meetings, they continued to be concerned but delightful and cooperative, and Alla continued with "DIR in the larger ecological context." Slowly, Raymond began to change. Raymond has gone from strolling up and down the aisles of supermarkets hoping to run his gaze along the needed item, to handling multiple shopping lists, navigating his way from store to store, looking for the shortest and fastest route, attending to how much time he has left with the understanding that if his and Alla's session ends because he had spent too much time looking at billboards or soap brands, and did not get the office supplies or sibling group snacks, he will not earn his quarters and then it will take him that much longer to earn money for a Miley Cyrus calendar or the ticket to the Empire State Building.

As weeks led into months, the time had come to show the staff how Raymond had changed, using this school-wide-known explosive case, as a guide for our intervention. We wanted to help staff in their slowing down, giving children time to think for themselves, looking for subtle cues to interpret their communicative attempts, taking into account the incredible processing challenges, and so on. Alla took a video camera, and recorded twenty minutes or so of Raymond's problem-solving, initiative-taking interaction. We called the staff together for at training on Friday afternoon, and Alla took the lead role. She stood up and rolled her video, she holding the camera focused on Raymond, while she spoke to and interacted with him. The stated purpose was to help the staff take a look at how they often overlooked early warning signs, antecedents, for the large behaviors that came later, in this case, Raymond's aggression. Since we believe at Rebecca School that every action is a communication of some sort, Alla approached the training as an opportunity to show the school what Raymond was communicating before he finally resorted to aggression. The video began.

Raymond's face filled the screen, and he and Alla spoke about what they were trying to accomplish. He was looking for something, and he moved about the school anxiously. His eyes flickered up and down. Alla stopped the video and pointed out to the staff that this was a moment of anxiety and confusion for Raymond. She walked them through the things that she and Raymond had just done, and what his sensory challenges and processing challenges were at that moment. She knew that the look on his face meant that he was about to lash out, so she offered him a way to ameliorate his anxiety, and took some of the pressure off him. In this way, she avoided his hitting or scratching her. He mentioned that he would like a snack, and that he would like popcorn particularly. "Notice what time he says this. Let's see how long it takes him to get back to his objective, and let's see how long it takes him to formulate and execute a plan." For the next few minutes, Raymond moved, apparently aimlessly, around the school. Alla followed him into my office at one point, and he focused on the schedules on the wall. Alla explains, "This is Raymond self-regulating. I often hear children being told to take deep breathes or take a few jumps on the trampoline to help with regulation, and those are very nice techniques, however those come from us, from the outside, those are not internalized and actually *self*-regulating. Counting to ten may slow Raymond down, but it does nothing for creating a calm secure feeling within. However, looking at schedules is a self-regulating method that Raymond came up with that works for him and that needs to be honored and understood."

Finally, after three-and-a-half minutes, Raymond said, "Popcorn," and headed to the snack cabinet. Alla stopped the video. "It took him all that time to process what he wanted, to figure out the plan, and to put it into action. If I had been worried about the final outcome, if it had made any difference to me whether he got the popcorn or not, if I had prompted him to hurry the process, he would not have had the time he needed to work through it himself. The thinking is the work, and the final product really doesn't matter at all." Alla was merely presenting her "taking Floortime to larger ecological context" methodology, but with the video of Raymond, with her obvious love and caring, and his obvious great struggle, it made for very compelling and emotional viewing. Here was the documentary evidence that this child, who had become a lightning rod for many of the passions in the school, was making real progress, long-term progress, in the way that he thought. Alla's presentation was so clear that others in the staff could see that it was possible to get kids to do the work, that the product really did not matter, and that thinking was the goal. Many in the staff were moved to tears, and the school changed a little that day, for the better.

At the time of this writing, it is two months after that presentation. Raymond has reentered a class, although not the classroom he left. He is calmer, does not attack people, indeed, restrains himself despite his stated desire to pull hair, and has become an active participant in the two classrooms over which he splits his time. He continues with Alla, continues to earn money for his shopping trips, and recently decided to spend his earnings on a pair of 2009 glasses, like the kind you would wear on New Year's Eve in Times Square to watch the ball drop. He was tremendously proud of these glasses, and told everyone that he looked like a star in them. He held his hands in a hard rock, "party-on," posture, and stuck out his tongue while waiting for people to take his picture. He had gone from the kid who staff feared in the hall, to the exuberant kid with the rock-star fantasy that everyone wanted to see and laugh with.

Our meetings with the parents continue. Now, when we speak, the parents can talk about their dreams for their son. They wonder if there is a higher educational format that will allow him to use his great intelligence after he graduates from Rebecca School. They have begun to look with some optimism, cautiously, to the future. Dad mentions something to me that he finds peculiar. "Raymond asked me for a watch, so I got one for him. It seems strange to me." Here was a boy who could keep time to the minute in his head. Somehow, what we did for him made it possible for him to consider giving up this continual counting to control his anxiety. He had begun to consider telling time like the rest of us mortals.

I told Dad, "I'm glad you got him the watch. Maybe, with luck and hard work, someday he will actually need it."

# Glossary

This glossary is purely to help you negotiate some of the jargon you might find in this book. I created it from a number of sources to make the book easier to read, but there may be definitions with which others might disagree. If there are mistakes of fact or inference, I apologize. You should consult more definitive sources if you want more information.

### Glossary of Terms

*Affect*: Emotion, intent, or desire. "Raise the level of affect" refers to bringing the child into greater enjoyment or heightened pleasure. The brain imprints things more efficiently when those things occur at "high affect."

*Auditory Processing*: The capacities involved in processing and interpreting auditory information, or what the brain does with what we hear. These capacities can include: the ability to pay attention to the spoken word (e.g., to pick out a person's voice from background noise), the ability to hear differences in sounds (e.g., "pat" vs. "pack"), the ability to remember what is heard, and the ability to comprehend what is heard (e.g., understand grammar).

*Circle of Communication*: One completed cycle of response between a child and another person in which the behavior and ideas of one person (verbally and/or nonverbally) are connected to those of the other person: the communication can be gestures, visual (eye contact), verbal, or a combination.

*Developmental Level*: A method of observing how children achieved particular developmental milestones, particularly those related to a child's ability to stay engaged, express mutual pleasure and attention, to engage in complex problem solving and symbolic play, and to link ideas.

*Dysregulation*: The state of being not available for engagement and inter-action, either by being too high or too low, physically and emotionally.

*Echolalia*: The repetition of words or phrases.

*Engagement*: Children coo, smile, and gesture with their partners. Building intimacy, joy, and a rhythm to interactions. The foundation for more purposeful interactions and learning.

*Expressive Language*: Capacities and abilities involved in both verbally and nonverbally communicating one's thoughts, feelings, desires, and needs to others.

*Fine-Motor Abilities*: The ability to use hands to manipulate small items (e.g., pinching, grasping, pencil and scissors use, and handwriting).

*Functional Emotional Developmental Levels or Milestones*: Refers to the emotional development of the child categorized by tasks and goals. The basic DIR model has six levels. They are:

I. Ability for regulation and shared attention.
II. Ability to form relationships, attachment, and engagement.
III. Ability to conduct two-way, purposeful communication.
IV. Ability to problem solve, use gestures in a continuous flow, and sup-port a complex sense of self.
V. Ability to use ideas representationally and functionally.
VI. Ability to build logical bridges between ideas and emotional thinking.

Three more levels were added to the DIR/Floortime model to promote more advanced reflective and abstract thinking. In order, they are:

VII. Ability to engage in multi-cause, comparative, and triangular thinking (e.g., "I feel left out when Susie likes Janet better than me.")
VIII. Ability to differentiate emotional gray-area thinking (e.g., ability to describe feelings about anger, love, excitement, love, and disap-pointment, as in, "I feel a little annoyed.")
IX. Ability to support intermittent reflective thinking, a stable sense of self, and an internal standard (e.g., "It's not like me to feel so angry," or "I shouldn't feel this jealous.")

**Gross-Motor Abilities**: The ability to use the whole body to execute large muscle movements (e.g., running, jumping, skipping, climbing).

**Individualized Education Program (IEP)**: A document describing the agreed-upon services a school will provide to a child with a disability (ages 3–21).

**Motor Planning**: The ability to formulate the idea of an action, organize it, and then execute it.

**Occupational Therapist**: Licensed therapist helps people develop the "skills for the job of living" necessary for independent and satisfying lives. Many OTs are trained in Sensory Integration therapy.

**Proprioceptive**: Sense of body awareness created by interpreting the information from the muscles and joints.

**Receptive Language**: Capacities involved in understanding the thoughts, feelings, desires, and needs of others. This includes the ability to interpret both verbal and nonverbal information from others.

**Reciprocal Interaction**: You hit the verbal and/or nonverbal "ball" to the child and the child "hits it back" with a response directly related to your words and/or actions. An initial goal of Floortime would be to have these reciprocal interactions be joyful and to sustain them for as long as possible.

**Regulation**: A state of calmness and an ability to attend to others as well as the environment.

**Scripting**: Refers to the child using a heavy emphasis on quotes from books or videos. Such a string of quotes may be used while reenacting a story, or to communicate a gestalt language chunk. Other times, a quote may just pop out at unexpected times.

**SEIT**: Special Education Itinerate Teacher. Usually, a one-on-one teacher assigned to a student to help them manage the difficulties of a less-restrictive academic environment.

**Sensory Defensiveness**: The inability of the body to accurately process information from the environment; produced by an oversensitivity to sensory stimuli. There is a constant state of "flight or fight" in one or many of these senses. For example, a child who is not sensory defensive might just cover his ears when there is a loud noise; a child who is sensory defensive might just disappear inside of himself instead.

**Sensory Integration**: The neurological ability to process and organize information that is gathered through our senses (the sensory information that is gathered from our bodies and our environment). Solid sensory integration means that each of the seven senses (visual, auditory, tactile, gustatory, olfactory, proprioceptive, and vestibular) works well and at the appropriate developmental level, and also that they work well together. Some individuals with ASD, who are articulate in describing their sensory integration difficulties, talk about their difficulty in using more than one avenue of sensory information at a time. For example, they have difficulty hearing when they are moving about.

**Sensory Modulation**: The ability to effectively organize and manage sensory information. A child's OT/SI therapist can give very specific strategies to ensure that the child's sensory system is well modulated and regulated. Children cannot benefit as well from Floortime if their bodies are so uncomfortable that they need to run or jump, or they cannot tolerate noise or touch.

**Shared Attention and Meaning**: Child and play partner are both focused on the same theme, object, and/or idea.

**Thinking Goes to School**: Furth, H.G., and Wachs, H. *Thinking Goes to School. Piaget's Theory in Practice*. New York: Oxford University Press, 1974.

Harry Wachs and Hans Furth designed a curriculum called *Thinking Goes to School*. Part of the program's mission was to "develop the habit of creative independent thinking," a goal it achieves largely through games—movement games, visual games, auditory games, and logic games. Rebecca School employs this curriculum throughout the school, and, particularly in its visual-spatial components, it is an integral part of the school program.

**Two-Way Communication (Gestural)**: The ability to have an emotional dialogue. The parent takes an interest in and responds to the child, and the child responds with gestural and verbal reactions.

**Vestibular Sense**: The "movement sense." This sense is involved in balance and position in space as well as muscle tone.

**Visual Processing**: Taking visual information from the environment, accurately interpreting the visual information, and using the information to make decisions for ideas and actions. Issues of visual processing are many and varied, and require a very specific diagnosis. Some children may also have some visual strengths that can be used effectively, making a specific diagnosis very important.

The ability to organize visual information and use it for performance in the environment (e.g., when throwing a softball to a friend, know how far away the friend is and how hard and how far to throw the ball). Well-developed visual-spatial abilities are also important for many aspects of mathematics and science as these abilities often depend on the ability to visualize complex theories. Children with weak visual-spatial processing abilities may have difficulty in following directions or reading comprehension because they are unable to mentally construct an image in their mind for either of these tasks.

# Acronyms

| | |
|---|---|
| **ABA** | Applied Behavior Analysis |
| **ADHD** | Attention Deficit Hyperactivity Disorder |
| **ASD** | Autism Spectrum Disorder |
| **CT** | Computed Tomography Scan |
| **DIR** | Developmental, Individual-Difference, Relationship-Based Model |
| **EEG** | Electroencephalogram |
| **FMRI** | Functional Magnetic Resonance Imaging |
| **GI** | Gastrointestinal |
| **ICDL** | Interdisciplinary Council on Developmental and Learning Disorders |
| **IEP** | Individual Education Plan |
| **MRI** | Magnetic Resonance Imaging |
| **NICU** | Neonatal Intensive Care Unit |
| **NIH** | National Institutes of Health |
| **NIMH** | National Institutes of Mental Health |
| **OCD** | Obsessive-Compulsive Disorder |

| | |
|---|---|
| **OT** | Occupational Therapy |
| **PECS** | Picture Exchange Communication System |
| **PET** | Positron Emission Tomography |
| **PT** | Physical therapy |
| **SEIT** | Special-Education Itinerate Teacher |
| **SI** | Sensory Integration |

CPSIA information can be obtained at www.ICGtesting.com
Printed in the USA
LVOW041926171111

255456LV00001B/142/P